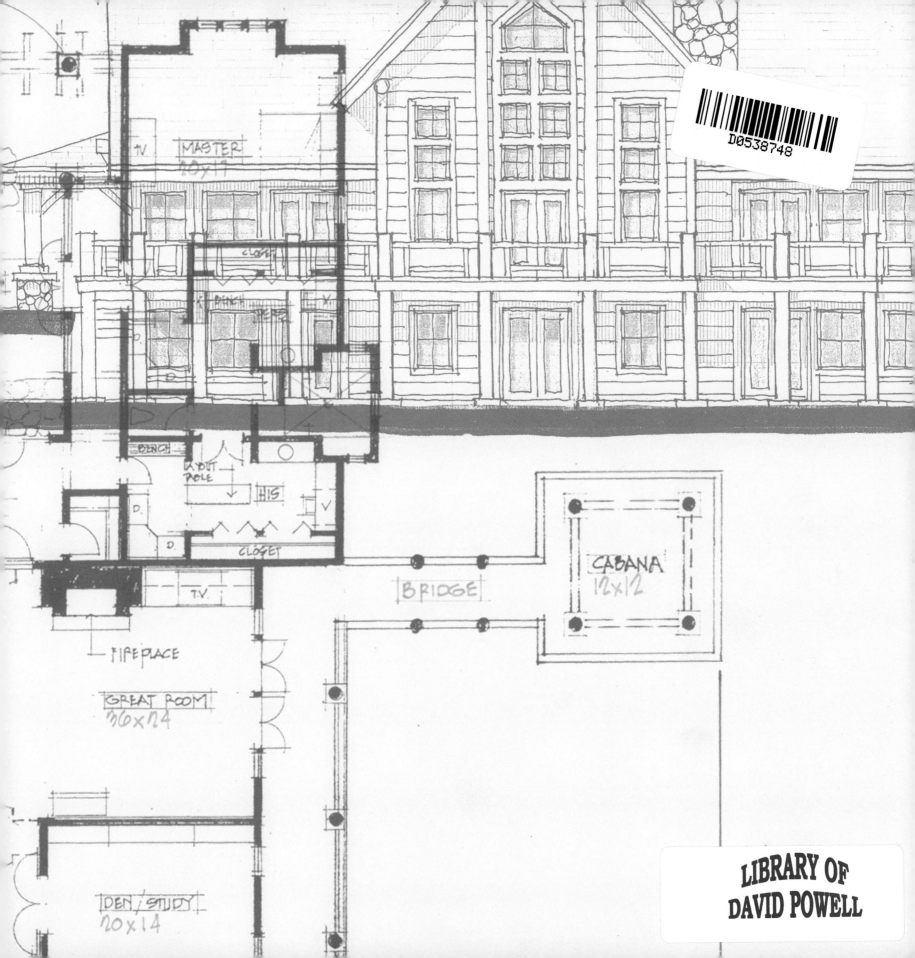

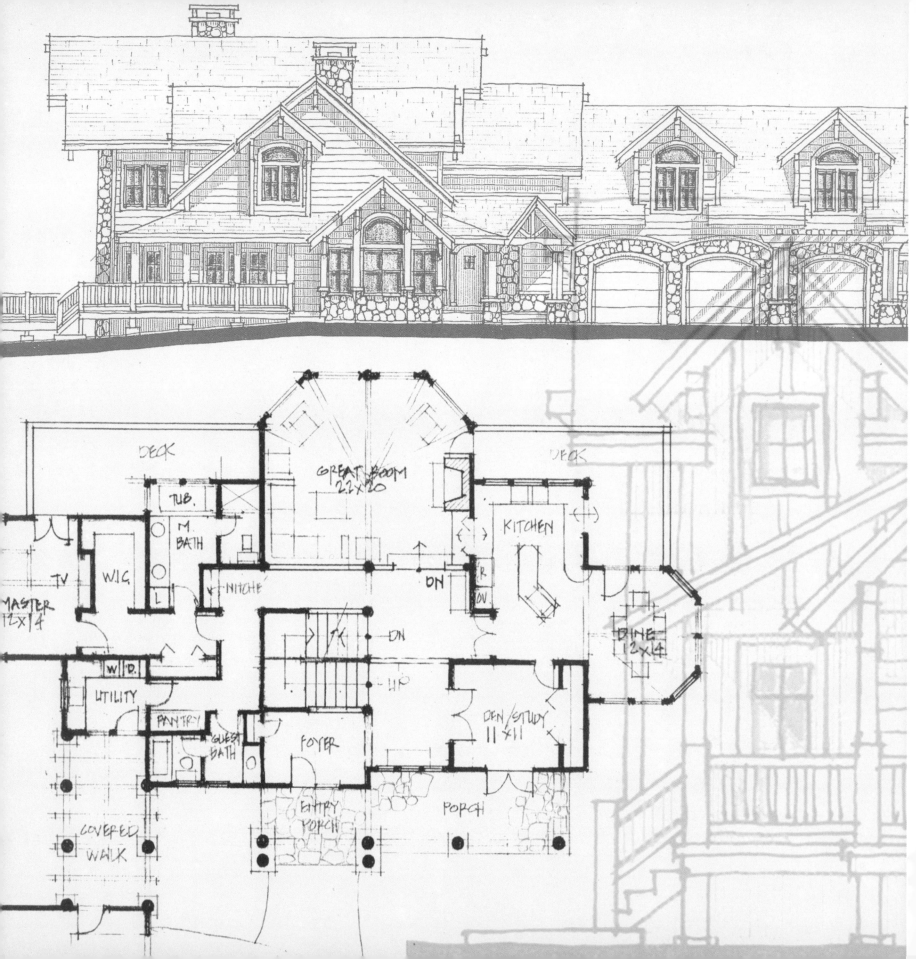

The Arts & Crafts Cabin

The Arts & Crafts Cabin

ROBBIN OBOMSAWIN

PHOTOGRAPHS BY
ROGER WADE

Gibbs Smith, Publisher
Salt Lake City

First Edition

08 07 06 05   5 4 3 2

Text © 2004 Robbin Obomsawin
Photographs © 2004 Roger Wade
Hand-drawn illustrations pages: v, xii, 25,
45–53, 144–45 © Alpenglow. Home designs
featured in this book are for sale through
MountainHomeDesigns.com.

Published by
Gibbs Smith, Publisher
P.O. Box 667
Layton, Utah 84041

Orders: 1-800-748-5439
www.gibbs-smith.com

Designed and produced by Steven Rachwal
Printed and bound in Hong Kong

**Library of Congress
Cataloging-in-Publication Data**

Obomsawin, Robbin, 1960-
The arts & crafts cabin / Robbin
Obomsawin ; photographs by Roger
Wade.—1st ed.   p. cm.
ISBN 1-58685-415-1
1. Log cabins. 2. Architecture,
Domestic—United States.
3. Decoration and ornament, Rustic—
United States. 4. Arts and crafts
movement—Influence. I. Title:
Arts and crafts cabin. II. Title.
NA8470 .O248 2004
728.7'3—dc22

2003024953

Photo credits and resources for design and building professionals who contributed to the
photographs within *The Arts & Crafts Cabin:*

Pages 2, 40, 42, 118
Alpine Log Homes, Victor, MT, 406-642-3451

**Pages 6, 10, 18, 30, 36, 42–43, 64–66, 69, 77–79,
86–91, 93, 95, 109L, 114, 117, 121–23, 126B,
137, 148B, 151, 153B, 154**
Locati Architects, Bozeman, MT, 406-587-1139

**Pages 10, 18, 30, 36, 42–43, 64, 66, 77, 90–91,
93, 95, 109L, 114, 117, 137, 148B, 151, 153B**
SBC, Inc., Bozeman, MT, 406-585-0735

Pages 10, 18, 30
Brooks Interior Design, Maitland, FL,
    407-539-2655

Pages 9, 94, 149, 152
Timberpeg, West Lebanon, NH, 440-338-4008

Pages 14, 54, 105, 116, 142
Sierra Timberframers, Nevada City, CA,
    530-292-9449

Pages 16, 26–27, 38, 81, 131, 133, 141
Mountain Timber Design, Golden, CO,
    303-278-8986

Pages 17, 101L
Danny Eagan Architect, Inc., Jackson, WY,
    307-733-8821

Pages 17, 101L
E. K. Reedy Interiors, Jackson, WY, 307-739-9121

Pages 18, 37, 98, 150
Wind River Timberframes, Inc., Mancos, CO,
    970-533-2007

**Pages 22, 34, 58, 67, 73, 84, 107, 128, 129,
139–40, 153T, 155**
Riverbend Timber Framing, Blissfield, MI,
    517-486-4355

Page 19
Mark Lowell Brown Architecture, Jackson, WY,
    307-733-1878

Pages 29, 96, 99, 101R, 108, 130, 135
Town & Country Cedar Homes, Petosky, MI,
    231-347-4360

Pages 32, 132, 136, 138, 148T
Baukunst Company, Bozeman, MT, 406-587-1080

Pages 32, 132, 136, 138, 148T
Sala Architects, Minneapolis, MN, 612-379-3037

Pages 35, 37, 71, 76, 146–47
The Ford Company, Kalispell, MT, 406-755-5224

Pages 39, 72–73, 102–3, 115, 121
Reichstetter Construction, Big Sky, MT,
    406-995-4460

Pages 39, 72–73, 102–3, 115
Van Bryan Studio Architects, Bozeman, MT,
    406-586-4777

Page 41
Sherry Grimes Design, Bonner, MT, 406-244-3605

Pages 44, 124
Old Style Log Works, Columbia Falls, MT,
    406-892-4665

Pages 56, 80, 83, 92L, 100
Mill Creek Post & Beam, Saluda, NC,
    828-749-8000

Pages 56–57, 61, 126T
Mindy Nichols Interiors, Kalispell, MT

Pages 62–63, 92R, 118
The Old World Cabinet Co., Whitefish, MT,
    406-862-3035

Pages 62–63, 97
Bigfork Builders, Bigfork, MT, 406-837-3373

Pages 62–63, 97, 109R
The Artisans, Kalispell, MT, 406-756-9737

Pages 62–63, 97
Interiors by Catherine, Inc., Kalispell, MT,
    406-755-4698

Page 65
Blue Ribbon Builders, Big Sky, MT, 406-995-4579

Pages 68, 104
Dynia Architects, Jackson, WY, 307-733-3766

Pages 74–75
Honka Log Homes, Evergreen, CO, 303-679-0568

Pages 78–79
Design Associates, Bozeman, MT, 406-582-8979

Pages 78–79
Ridgeline Builders, Bozeman, MT, 406-587-1925

Page 82
Charles Stuhlberg Interiors, Ketchum, ID,
    208-726-4568

Pages 85, 113
Oakbridge Timber Framing, Howard, OH,
    740-599-5711

Pages 92R, 109R, 118
LaChance Builders, Whitefish, MT, 406-862-5597

Pages 119, 120, 127
Maple Island Log Homes, Suttons Bay, MI,
    231-271-4042

Contents

Acknowledgments

OVER THE YEARS, I HAVE MET SO MANY WONDERFUL LOG BUILDERS, DESIGN PROFESSIONALS, AND HOMEOWNERS WHO HAVE SUCH A PASSION FOR FINDING THE BALANCE BETWEEN QUALITY AND THOUGHTFUL DESIGN. MANY TRADITIONAL LOG-JOINERY METHODS WERE OPENLY AND UNSELFISHLY SHARED BY MEMBERS OF THE INTERNATIONAL LOG BUILDERS' ASSOCIATION. AFTER THE LONG WEEKEND OF LECTURES AT THE ANNUAL INTERNATIONAL LOG BUILDERS' ASSOCIATION, I BECAME OVERWHELMED AND SCARED SPITLESS, FEELING LIKE I WOULD NEVER BE ABLE TO ACHIEVE THE LEVEL OF KNOWLEDGE THAT SO MANY OF THE INNOVATIVE AND CREATIVE LOG BUILDERS POSSESSED. BUT THERE WAS ALWAYS SOMEONE WILLING TO TAKE US UNDER THEIR WING TO MAKE IT ALL FEEL LESS INTIMIDATING. FOR ALL THIS, I AM SO GRATEFUL!

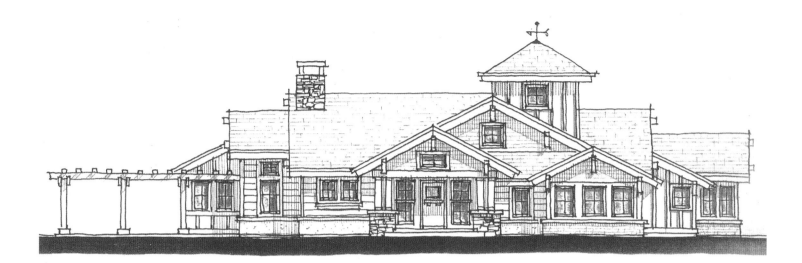

To my clients, who have been so wonderful and inspirational in their enthusiasm, love of life, and love of architecture, we have very much enjoyed building your dreams! It has been such a pleasure to be able to share similar interests. I have to say that there is something about the individuals who want handcrafted log work; they are so passionate about the journey and research that is required to build their dreams.

I would also like to mention the very few clients from hell who will always be remembered because they taught me more than I care to know. Those projects have become an accelerated form of learning where much of the information of what *not* to do is shared so others can learn from their construction dyslexia.

I thank my publisher, Mr. Gibbs Smith, for his wonderful support. It is so fun to see the light in his eyes as he is always looking for the latest and best for his book collections to share with the world. I truly appreciate his support of women within the industry, let alone this labor-intensive form of artistry that is so often overlooked or unappreciated.

To my editor, Suzanne Taylor, and all her assistants, who are each and every one a part of building this book, I thank you for the freedom you have allowed me and the guidance and support you have given, along with getting me to the airport at ungodly hours!

Thanks to Marty and Jim Wheeler of Alpenglow Mountain Home Designs, who supplied most of the drawings within this book. Design professionals are often undervalued within this business and deserve more respect, especially when they are so dedicated and talented. Some design professionals are so passionate and involved in their projects, and it is fun to find individuals like these to share with the public. With their magic pens, they can make a project come to life.

Thanks to Roger Wade, whose photography has always stood out and who has done so much in documenting the work of handcrafters and architecture for more than eighteen years. His work shows such a mix of hard work, long days on the road, and determination. Roger's driven dedication to the world of architectural photography is captured on film for generations to enjoy. I have to stop all my work when Roger's photos come in. I get lost in time and forget all my urgent appointments and meetings once those boxes of film come to my office door.

The curved wall and windows of the far room are a great contrast to the massive squared timbers that make up the skeleton of this home's frame.

Introduction

THE OLD FORM AND PHILOSOPHY OF THE ARTS & CRAFTS STYLE IS THE INSPIRATION FOR CLASSIC, TIMELESS DESIGN THAT IS MAKING HISTORY ONCE MORE AND REGAINING THE PROMINENCE AND POPULARITY IT ONCE ENJOYED AT THE TURN OF THE CENTURY. THE ARTS & CRAFTS FORM OF DESIGN STILL SPEAKS TO US TODAY AND CONTINUES TO INFLUENCE A NEW GENERATION OF ARCHITECTS AND CRAFTSMEN.

The Arts & Crafts Cabin was created to share some of the new forms of construction that have become the perfect blend of handcrafted log-joinery skills merged with the Arts & Crafts principles and philosophy of the modern-day craftsman. Pure simplicity and natural imperfections of raw logs are beautiful contrasts to other natural or man-made materials. The new hybrid style of Arts & Crafts creates an exterior punctuated by the warmth of log elements where logs breathe life into the home's structure, creating once again, over a hundred years later, a new hybrid of Arts & Crafts architectural style that aesthetically blurs the line between indoors and out.

"Eyebrow" arches are cut into the base of this double-timber collar tie. A mix of stone, wood and glass were skillfully designed to create a comfortable feel. This cabin is a testament to the importance of an experienced design professional.

The traditional form of a hand-crafted log artisan's skill lends itself well to the philosophy of the Craftsman-style home. The massive log columns, combined with beautifully and skillfully crafted round and square log trusses, highlight the home's form. The architectural accents of log elements add distinction and permanence to a home's frame. The structure's exterior façade of log elements can easily be mixed with wood shingles, rough-sawn boards, cedar clapboards, stone walls, stucco walls, or a combination of many of these materials to give the home a depth of textures.

I have been so lucky to see such inspiring, quality handcrafted log construction and design talent over the years. I wanted to focus on some of the new and upcoming artists in the handcrafted trade with this book. The lush photographs captured by Roger Wade and the artful renderings drawn by brothers Jim and Marty Wheeler will give you a glimpse of just a small fraction of what can be created with this style of architecture where some of its forms are still within its infancy.

The Arts & Crafts Cabin features and celebrates some of the brilliant photography of Roger Wade, one of the industry's premier photographers, whose classic style has chronicled the work of handcrafted log construction and timber joinery over many years. Roger's luminous style has captured the essence of log and timber structures with dynamic compositions, striking interpretations of space,

skillful lighting, and artful styling that, without words, inspire us all.

The most innovative log-and-timber hybrid designs I have come across in the last few years are the Wheeler brothers' interpretation of Arts & Crafts bungalows. Some of these designs, merged with traditional log-joinery methods, are giving birth to hybrid forms of North American log-joinery and traditional timber architecture. The designs of their craftsman and bungalow homes show great sensitivity to their flow and function, with every detail considered.

Home building is a large and ever-changing market where hard work and many years of dedication often go unnoticed or are easily diluted with the masses of buildings that are all "sizzle with no beef." It often becomes hard for many to differentiate between all the slick furnishings, marketing, advertising, and lush, cropped photography that can cloud the true "bones" of construction, camouflaging the structural reality.

The following examples of the history and philosophy of Arts & Crafts style are only guidelines and inspiration for those who prefer a more contemporary form of architecture. The American bungalow is a practical approach to living in its simplest form. Its attention to detail and use of quality materials and craftsmanship are ideal for those who despise the poor quality of mass production, where the home is built to last only the length of its mortgage. We search for some of those same principles and values that the craftsman philosophy and style of home focused around—hearth, home, and family.

It is the combination of not only the design but also the artisans or craftsmen involved that creates the magic of a project's final outcome. Recently someone told me that they had once read that "a builder is a person who builds with his hands; the craftsman is the person who builds with his hands and mind; and the artisan is the person who builds with his hands, mind, and soul." I hope these floor plans and design ideas will contain the artistry and soul that will inspire you and be a catalyst to pave the way to home design that captures passion, love of life, and respect of today's handcrafted builders.

The Arts & Crafts Movement
of the 1800s

THROUGHOUT THE EARLY AND MID-1800s, THE MAJORITY OF AMERICAN ARCHITECTURE WAS DERIVED FROM CLASSIC EUROPEAN FORMS OF ARCHITECTURE. THE VICTORIAN STYLES OF DESIGN, SUCH AS QUEEN ANNE, HAD BECOME VERY POPULAR DURING THIS PERIOD. VICTORIAN HOMES FEATURED EXTREME MATERIAL CONTRASTS AND A VARIETY OF ARCHITECTURAL STYLES. THESE WERE FLAVORED WITH VIBRANT, BOLD COLORS AND BUSY WALLPAPER PATTERNS. THE VICTORIAN/QUEEN ANNE ERA WAS KNOWN FOR ITS EXTENSIVE USE OF EXTERIOR EMBELLISHMENTS, INCLUDING TURRETS, IRONWORK, DETAILED MOLDINGS, WOOD CARVINGS, DECORATIVE SPINDLES, GINGERBREAD PATTERNS, AND FRETWORK.

Flared-base stone columns and low-pitch flared roof systems expose the structural elements that are pure in simplicity, tying the home to its outdoor surroundings.

Many well-known architects of the time rebelled against such rigid formality and what they considered useless ornamental excess. Frank Lloyd Wright, Gustav Stickley, and Charles and Henry Greene all greatly contributed to transforming old architectural design standards into a new form of American-based design as each developed his own signature style. This new pioneering design was coined "Arts & Crafts." The Arts & Crafts movement started in Europe but was adopted by many American design professionals of the time. The style was simple, bold, and practical, and met the new requirements of what was then considered a modern lifestyle. The design components provided a strong contrast to the assembly-line factory system of machined and processed materials of the day.

Mission-style, slat-back chairs balance the rhythm of the overhead timber-frame trusses. Notice the slight underside arch of the upright column and knee brace.

THE PHILOSOPHY

The primary inspiration of the Arts & Crafts movement was nature. It was borrowed from and captured by using local or indigenous materials and traditional art forms. Using American craftspeople was central to the Arts & Crafts design concept. The craftspeople constructed homes using traditional iron and/or copper blacksmithing techniques, pottery, and weavings as their media. These traditional craft styles were used by skilled carpenters to produce a less processed and more natural architectural design base.

A spiritual connection to nature, coupled with the use of more natural and handcrafted materials, created a home that would better blend into its surrounding environment. The designer's ultimate goal was that a home should be a sanctuary away from urban factories, where people primarily worked at that time. The Arts & Crafts movement was conceived

The formation and pattern of square timbers create strong lines and a sense of permanence within this structure. Large-scale chandeliers were added to help fill the open space created by the high vaulted ceilings.

ABOVE: Carved into the home's structure, this kitchen becomes fluid in the home's design. Arts & Crafts–style lighting, cabinetry, and accents of oversized log elements add architectural punch.

Adding a truss and timber columns will draw the eye and welcome all that enter.

to create harmony with nature and to provide a meditative charm, or Zen-ness, in order to bring peace and tranquility to all who entered an Arts & Crafts home.

Over time, Arts & Crafts homes became more modest in size but never lacked in functionality or flow. The floor plans were designed without quarters for maids, nannies, or servants.

The open designs were also more conducive to family interaction. They were planned to create a functional workspace where the fireplace, or hearth, would become the family center. Because of the introduction of central heat sources, the fireplace had more flexibility than before. It could now be used solely for its beautiful and mesmerizing characteristics.

The whole emphasis of an Arts & Crafts–style home was to create a well-crafted structure with less-processed materials as close to their natural state as possible. This simplified design style appealed to the tastes and pocketbooks of first-time home buyers, the middle class, and working-class people.

The combination and joinery methods within whole-log and timber-frame work are endless, limited only by one's imagination.

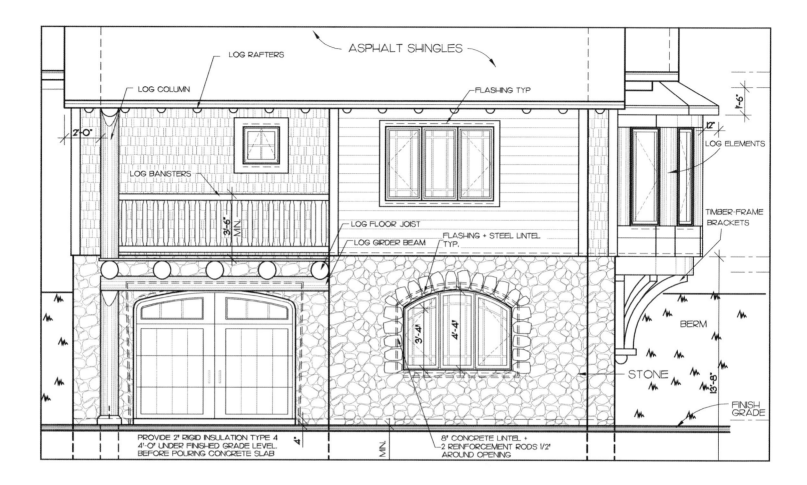

ASPHALT SHINGLES

LOG RAFTERS

LOG COLUMN

FLASHING TYP

LOG ELEMENTS

LOG BANISTERS

TIMBER-FRAME BRACKETS

LOG FLOOR JOIST

LOG GIRDER BEAM

FLASHING + STEEL LINTEL TYP.

BERM

STONE

FINISH GRADE

PROVIDE 2" RIGID INSULATION TYPE 4 4'-0" UNDER FINISHED GRADE LEVEL. BEFORE POURING CONCRETE SLAB

MIN.

8" CONCRETE LINTEL + 2 REINFORCEMENT RODS 1/2" AROUND OPENING

2'-0"

3'-6" MIN.

3'-4"

4'-4"

4'

1'-6"

12"

13'-8"

THE DESIGN STYLES

The classic Arts & Crafts styles of the California Bungalow, Prairie, American Foursquare, and Craftsman incorporated similar design features. The homes were typically simple and free of excess ornamentation. Many of the homes were one to one-and-a-half stories high, featuring long, low-pitched, sloping, gabled rooflines.

These unusual rooflines displayed exposed rafters and braces along their wide gable ends and exaggerated roof eaves. The wide, sheltering overhangs visually "capped" the home, nesting it into the earth and its surroundings. The Craftsman and Bungalow architectural accents often featured a cobblestone foundation, porch pillars, and chimneys that broaden at their

bases. The rest of the home was constructed of wood clapboard or shingles finished in natural earth tones and shades of brown. Organic materials were often used in various combinations throughout the exterior design.

The use of many windows, including stained-glass and leaded-glass, flooded the rooms with natural light, making nature

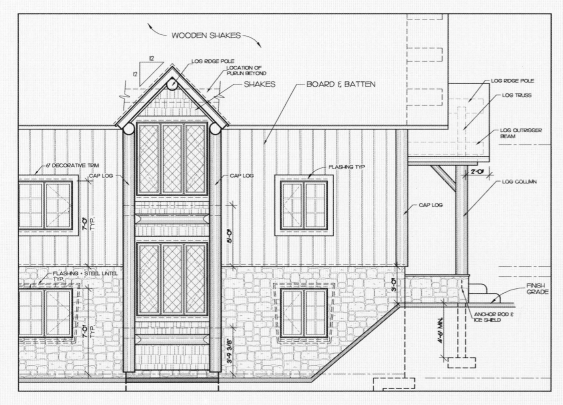

RIGHT: Cap logs add to this home's bump-out and house the stair system that climbs three stories.

OPPOSITE: Bumps and jogs, arched window tops, cottage-style window grilles and a mix of exterior textures are important elements in a Craftsman-style bungalow.

WOODEN SHAKES
LOG RIDGE POLE
LOCATION OF PURLIN BEYOND
SHAKES
BOARD & BATTEN
LOG RIDGE POLE
LOG TRUSS
LOG OUTRIGGER BEAM
6' DECORATIVE TRIM
CAP LOG
CAP LOG
FLASHING TYP
LOG COLUMN
CAP LOG
FLASHING • STEEL LINTEL TYP.
FINISH GRADE
ANCHOR ROD & ICE SHIELD

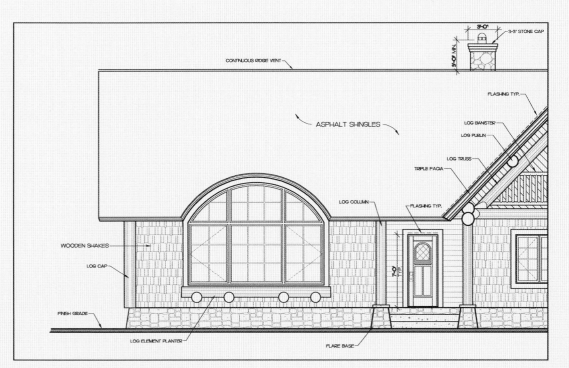

LEFT: The arch of the window is cut into the home's roofline, creating a barrel arch on the home's interior. Under the window a log is carved out as a planter that will cascade with color and trailing ivy. The front entry is bumped in to create a roof cover overhead.

CONTINUOUS RIDGE VENT
3'-3' STONE CAP
FLASHING TYP.
ASPHALT SHINGLES
LOG BANISTER
LOG PURLIN
LOG TRUSS
TRIPLE FACIA
LOG COLUMN
FLASHING TYP.
WOODEN SHAKES
LOG CAP
FINISH GRADE
LOG ELEMENT PLANTER
FLARE BASE

*These timber-frame log pergolas are designed to grow vines to form
a canopy of greens overhead. They also stand alone as an architectural accent.*

Clinker bricks are cast-offs that are positioned too close to the heat during the firing process in the kilns. The bricks become malformed and the colors become uneven in shades of dark red, brown, and black. This adds character to the bricks, giving them greater dimension and texture. Clinker bricks are sometimes used within the exterior base of a home's foundation veneers.

a part of the home's décor. The Craftsman and Bungalow design concept also used an abundance of outdoor living space with an oversized front porch and a rear patio. These porches and patios were often enhanced with a pergola or trellises that captured the rhythm of a simple pattern. The porches were typically wide, giving the feel of outside rooms. Off-kitchen outdoor dining areas were often incorporated into a plan and served as additional entertaining space.

Because of the tuberculosis epidemic and the health philosophy of the times, many homes were designed with "tuberculosis rooms," or sleeping porches, that were wrapped in windows and light. Pulmonary health specialists recommended that fresh, "healing" air should freely circulate throughout the structure.

The inglenook was a very popular design concept where a built-in seating area or benches were installed around or on each side of the hearth. The

fireplaces were utilitarian and built with local stone or clinker bricks.

In some of the more affluent homes, the fireplace might be embellished with decorative tiles and framed with clean-line wood mantels.

The Arts & Crafts–style homes used an abundance of woodwork that was usually squared and simpler than the Victorian styles, which flaunted excess gingerbread patterns and fret-

work. The woods were usually chosen for their quality of grain and were never intended to be painted. In particular, the quarter-sawn grain was featured and prized. Finely constructed wooden furniture, flooring, paneling, and built-ins such as window seats, dining nooks, bookshelves, cabinetry, and furniture were all standard accessories to the home's master design.

ABOVE: Today's heart of the home is in the kitchen. In this home we incorporate a modern inglenook with a fireplace that is raised for a better view from the table. The raised hearth also gives room for wood storage along with plenty of shelf area to set hot dishes.

Quarter-sawn oak is one of the hallmark woods used in many Arts & Crafts, Craftsman, and Prairie-style homes and furnishings. The quarter-sawn method of cutting creates a product that is structurally stronger, finer in grain, and less susceptible to warping and checking than "slab cut" methods used in the milling process. Quarter-sawing yields less lumber per tree and requires considerably more labor than standard sawing. During the milling process, the log is split into four quarters and then cut on the diagonal from the center of the tree out toward the edges. This method of sawing across the grain, particularly with oak, creates a very strong, well-defined graining, often referred to as the "rays." These rays run from the center of the tree outward. A quarter-sawn log results in wood with distinctive, decorative graining with a wavy pattern.

The Arts & Crafts home was designed specifically to feature a sense of space, an openness of the rooms, and the rustic or bold square styling that would have a completely different feel from the fussy cluttered style of Victorian homes of the era. Strong geometric lines created a contemporary feel, but the use of wood radiated warmth and comfort that only wood can do.

QUALITY VS. QUANTITY

One- or one-and-a-half-story bungalows were the first types of houses to be built and sold by contractors on a speculative basis. Because of the ease and simplicity of construction, this new form of architecture was perfect for the masses. Bungalows and other Craftsman houses could even be ordered, ready to assemble, through the Sears & Roebuck and Montgomery Ward catalogs. Blueprints were sold in many popular pattern books and magazines of the time. The original Craftsman and Bungalow concept of building with the finest craftsmanship and quality materials was eventually compromised by mass-marketing, quick turnaround building times, and shoddy or unskilled workmanship. This cheapened the "rules of form" and philosophy of the Arts & Crafts movement.

Arched timbers and flared base columns anchor the home's design.

AMERICAN-BASED DESIGNERS AND ARCHITECTS OF THE ARTS & CRAFTS MOVEMENT

The Arts & Crafts movement was most popular from about the late 1800s to approximately 1930. Craftsman and Bungalow were the dominant design styles for the smaller homes during this time. This American hybrid style spread across the country through pattern books and magazines, with each region creating its own unique interpretation and regional differences. The bold angular lines and stripped simplicity of Arts & Crafts design was a daring contrast to the more heavily machined styles of the Victorian era.

GUSTAV STICKLEY was an innovative designer and architect of the period. He was a major influence due to his creative designs and popular magazine, *The Craftsman*. Stickley had the talent to reduce a house or furnishings to simple forms. He was sensitive to designing structures that would harmonize with their surroundings by using low, broad roof proportions and minimizing the ornamentation, which in turn would give the structure a distinct character.

CHARLES AND HENRY GREENE, the American architect brothers, designed bungalows that were later dubbed the "Ultimate Bungalows," in Pasadena and other parts of California. The Greenes have been credited for popularizing the Bungalow style that grew out of the Craftsman/ Arts & Crafts style of design. They used a lot of post-and-beam framing and details within their architecture. The long, protruding timber rafter tails created a symphony of shadows with precise rhythmic flow within the roof eaves. Greene and Greene's style was a more open form of outdoor rooms and design that would take advantage of the temperate elements of California.

FRANK LLOYD WRIGHT took the Arts & Crafts style to new dimensions with his Prairie style of design that was based on the philosophy of "organic architecture." He believed that the core principle of building was to develop a structure out of its natural indigenous surroundings. His signature design style incorporated low exterior horizontal proportions and strong, horizontal projecting rooflines. Wright's bold originality was a radical approach to architectural design that is an inspiration to many architects of today.

ARTS & CRAFTS–STYLE FURNISHINGS

The Arts & Crafts home cannot be discussed without mentioning the furniture. The interior décor was just as much a part of the Arts & Crafts movement as the architectural floor plan. One of the early results of the movement in América was Mission furniture, first popularized by Gustav Stickley, who had tremendous insight and understanding of the movement. He wanted to create handcrafted furniture based on honesty and simplicity, with designs that would appeal to anyone. Stickley introduced his Craftsman line when he opened United Crafts in Eastwood, New York, in 1898. Stickley's innovative, simple designs always focused on the high-quality joinery that

ABOVE: High-back Mission chairs, built-in hutches, and rustic minimalism equal pure simplicity in the Arts & Crafts form of architecture.

NEXT PAGE: Arched rafter-style trusses, oversized purlins, and outrigger beams create a canopy of forest overhead. A flared column base has always been a signature detail of an Arts & Crafts–style bungalow. The metal turn buckle is not just a decoration but also a very important structural component that keeps the wall plum, so the outward thrust of the heavy roof system does not spread the top of the walls over time.

highlighted the craftsman's skills, with raw beauty being the cornerstone of the design base.

Gustav Stickley's brothers, Leopold and John George, also started their own furniture company in 1905 that still bears the family name. Their collection of Arts & Crafts furniture was, and still is, cherished for its quality and beautiful designs. It set the standard in fine American woodworking. The Stickleys' work ethics, insight, and practical application of the new inventions of factory lines, innovative employee profit sharing, and machinery were used to create more affordable furniture. They produced quality-constructed furnishings for the masses.

The Stickleys' designs were quite radical for the time, using bold framing with angular sculptural forms. The uses of translucent wood finishes were also an important part of their work; these finishes highlighted the quality of the chosen quarter-sawn wood graining. Special formulas for rustic finishes were also developed by Stickley and others to give the wood an aged appearance and luminous patina.

These quality-built furnishings are treasured for their classic style, clean lines, and contemporary feel. Older Craftsman or Mission furniture is among the most prized and sought after at auction houses and antiques galleries. The traditional Stickley furniture patterns are still being built today by a new owner, the Audis family, whose company carries on the tradition of pride, integrity, and deep respect for the Arts & Crafts heritage.

OTHER ARTISANS OF THE TIME

The 1800s was a time of great design experimentation and artistic inspirations that spawned new innovation in American architecture within the Arts & Crafts style. A new frontier of artistic expression bravely forged ahead, creating new and exciting design concepts. The growing popularity of the Arts & Crafts style created opportunities for upcoming artisans practicing "old trades," where more traditional hand-joinery techniques were used.

Artist colonies were formed to explore and promote the artisan's potential as homeowners sought for more contemporary architectural trimmings and interior designs. Copper and metalwork became a popular medium where the signature divots of the artisan's hammer were coveted and proudly featured. New styles of lighting fixtures were designed with simple lines and form. And contemporary lamps were sculpted in bronze and metals with mica shades that would illuminate the room in a soft natural light.

The New Age of Arts & Crafts Design

A long purlin supports the rafter-style roof system that is held by a system of upward posts with knee braces. These knee braces are mortised and tenoned into base-cord collar ties. The collar ties are not only beautiful but also structural components that keep the weight of the roof system from pushing the upper walls outward.

THE RENEWED INTEREST IN CRAFTSMAN- AND BUNGALOW-STYLE HOMES HAS INSPIRED A GROWING NUMBER OF ARCHITECTS TO SPECIALIZE IN THE DESIGN AND CONSTRUCTION OF HOMES IN KEEPING WITH THE ARTS & CRAFTS TRADITION. THIS TIME, THOUGH, THE HOUSES ARE NOT INEXPENSIVE OR OF A MODEST SIZE; THEY ARE OFTEN LARGER AND MORE ELABORATE THAN ORIGINAL ARTS & CRAFTS HOMES. HOWEVER, SOME HOMES ARE EMBRACING THE MORE MODEST BUT QUALITY-BUILT STRUCTURE, WHERE LESS IS MORE. THERE IS A RENAISSANCE UNDERWAY TO RECAPTURE A LESS TUMULTUOUS AND LESS COMPLICATED TIME. THERE IS ALSO AN INCREASED AWARENESS OF QUALITY JOINERY METHODS AND A RENEWED RESPECT FOR A GOOD CRAFTSMAN'S AND ARTISAN'S HONED SKILLS.

The log builder and timber framer of today have a long tradition that pre-dates Arts & Crafts architecture. Log building and quality log joinery is a process of construction that cannot be rushed or forced. The log craftsman's skill takes years to develop and his experience will ensure a strong contrast

Today a new hybrid of log-element construction is emerging where whole round logs are used in a post-and-beam style of log joinery (see pages 59, 120, 123, 124, and 127).

and sculptural form to the home's basic design.

The new forms of log-element hybrid structures provide an interesting twist to the old form of Craftsman and Bungalow architecture. The lines, design content, and philosophy are the signature items that form the Arts & Crafts design base of a log-element structure, where strength is gained by adding large-diameter log timbers that create mass and visual weight in the structure.

OPPOSITE: The log ceiling joists are parallel timbers that support the floor or roof system above. Their size and spacing will be determined by the spans and weight loads above.

RIGHT: Curved railings are constructed in the Arts & Crafts pattern, with oversized log timbers stained dark to contrast with the white of the walls.

Log elements add a new dimension that creates rustic drama to the home's overall form. Log elements may also be added to the home's interior to help soften and/or divide indoor spaces. Log trusses, floor/ceiling joists, stairs, fireplace mantels, railings, upright columns, and more can be incorporated as log elements. The interior design can lean toward the rustic or the more modern and contemporary, depending upon your personal preferences.

Log-element details can be whatever you make them. The sky is the limit. It is the one style that can be enjoyed by a minimalist or a collector, a traditionalist or an individual with contemporary or minimal tastes. It is a base of style and architecture from which to be inspired. The end result will reflect a combination of your taste, your design professional's years of experience, and the individual con-

LEFT: *Using antique furnishings in new construction will help warm and soften the structure. Here, a beautiful antique cupboard is used to hold extra linens and supplies.*

BELOW: *Log-element structures may have very little log work within a given area. The amount of log work required, budgeted, or designed can vary greatly.*

OPPOSITE: *The mix of iron, stone, wood, and glass are skillfully designed to combine manmade and natural materials. Technology combined with the skills of artisans and craftspeople give us a broad range of great talent and techniques to choose from.*

ABOVE: *This piece-on-piece, square-cut log shell has Craftsman-style outrigger braces in the gable ends and doubled tail rafters that create a rhythm of pattern over the entry porch as well as within all rafter overhangs.*

OPPOSITE: *Arts & Crafts–style entry doors, side lights, railings, lamps, and furnishings were added by expert craftsmen using quality materials.*

struction methods of the artisans you choose. The log-element hybrid style works well in single-family residential homes, townhouses, or commercial structures.

This form of log-element design also works well in renovations. It is truly amazing how log elements either sprinkled or poured throughout a well-designed renovation can transform a basic, average, or older structure into one with stunning architectural presence.

ARTS & CRAFTS DESIGN WITHIN LOG HOMES

THE ELEGANCE OF ADDED LOG ELEMENTS

Years of experience and an artistic flair can bring depth and interest to a home's character. Adding strong architectural elements can give a fresh look and appeal to an otherwise boring structure. With the aid of a well-trained and experienced designer you can always improve the curb appeal of a bland or dreary home. Even an average or quaint home can be transformed into a home of rustic elegance or storybook charm.

LEFT: Stunning accents of stained glass within the door and sidelights allow light to pour into the entry, where white walls also help reflect natural lighting. Just a hint of log on walls adds texture, which in turn gives depth to the impressive entrance.

OPPOSITE: Curved handrails and stairs are built with round-on-round connections "scarfed" down to square connections that appear to grow out of one another. Their simple and fluid appearance is an illusion; this technique requires years of experience to achieve.

BELOW: *Soft, sensual, whole-log ceiling-joist supports contrast with the squared railings and furniture of this home's décor.*

RIGHT: *This outdoor room is on the edge of nature; panoramic views wrap around the small, traditional, dovetail log cabin with Arts & Crafts details.*

Craftsman-style details can also be added to a handcrafted log home.

AREAS OF ADDED DESIGN POTENTIAL

We often spend a great deal of time with the interior of our homes and forget the home's exterior. Listed below are a few key areas that would enhance the exterior of your home as you work with an experienced and creative design professional:

- Balance exterior elements for overall curb appeal.
- Refine with subtle rustic log accents.
- Define your home's overall flow.
- Create better depth and dimension to a structure.
- Create a look that is out-of-the-ordinary.

ABOVE: To give the same structure more of an Arts & Crafts feel, the design professional took away the whole-log elements and added timber-frame truss-style rafters with cantilevered supports and decorative gable-end "web" pieces. The windows were changed to create an Arts & Crafts design. A large stone base was added with flared stone column supports that flank the entry door. The home's siding materials were changed on the garage wing to help break up the long lines and add texture to the overall design. (BEFORE)

BELOW: A home of log accents is highlighted with cap logs, upright columns and log rails. The main structure is symmetrical, with the addition of a garage wing to the right. (AFTER)

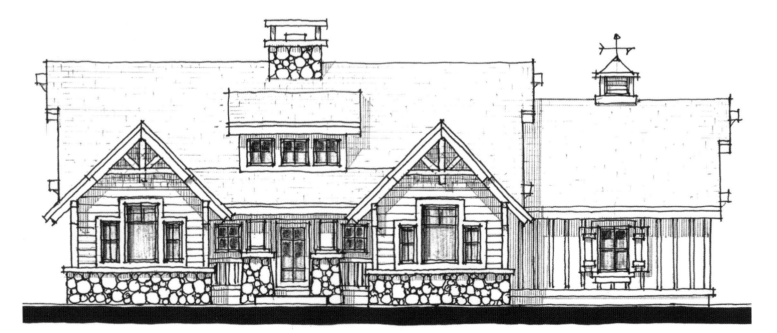

- Review the possibilities of exterior material choices and combinations.
- Add design elements like dormers and bump-outs, giving character or function to your home's plan.

- Better conceptualize the placement, design choices, and configurations of each window unit.
- Choose the best door for your home's overall design.

- If a garage was added to the blueprint, gauge how it will relate to your home's overall plan.
- Assess what type of garage door, window, and roof pitches will fit best with your home's design.

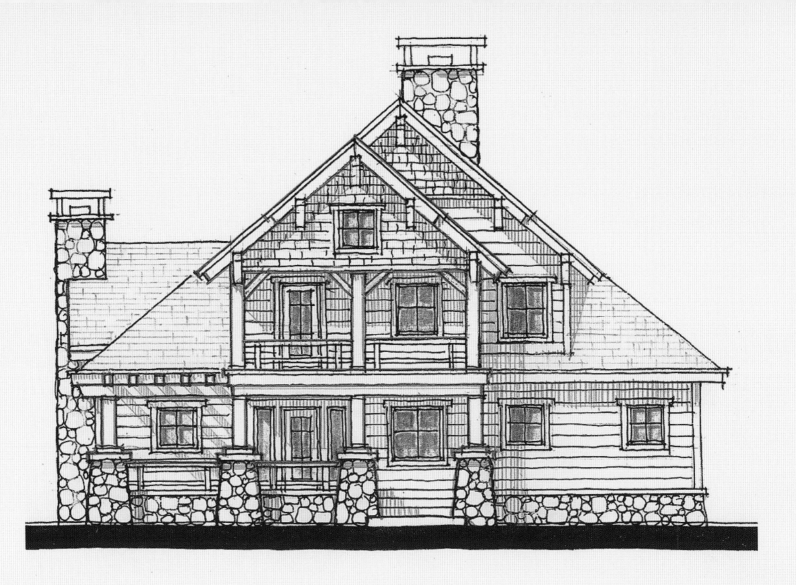

OPPOSITE: *This log-element structure is accented with large-diameter log columns, web trusses, and a porch railing with an oversized log as a top rail. (BEFORE)*

ABOVE: *This home was given strong Arts & Crafts detailing to create a different overall feel to the structure's exterior. A flared chimney stack, column bases, and foundation were added to the structure. Cube-style windows were installed along with an Arts & Crafts–style trim. The door's design and location were changed to better fit the home's floor plan. Squared timber outrigger beams were added to the roof's typical large overhangs. (AFTER)*

ABOVE AND LEFT: *This conventional structure is given Arts &*
Crafts personality by the use of massive log rafters, web details,
cubed windows, and combinations of window sizes with arched
top transoms. Changing the stone base materials to a larger
stone, and capping the tops of the columns with a large sheet of
granite (cut to shed the water), this home's exterior changes
dramatically. The artistry and experience of the designer is
evident in these transformations.(BEFORE AND AFTER)

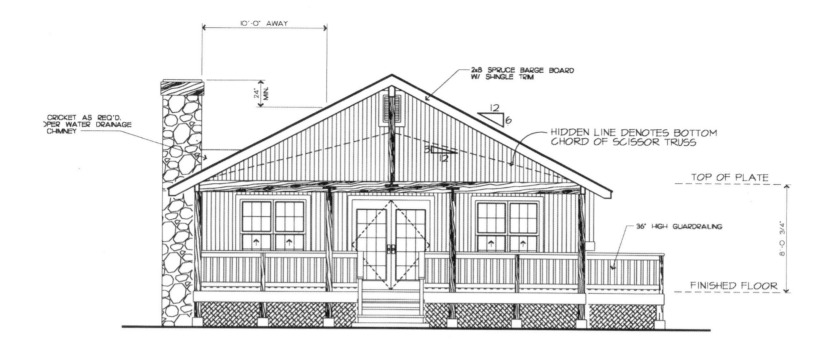

CRICKET AS REQ'D.
?PER WATER DRAINAGE
CHIMNEY

2x8 SPRUCE BARGE BOARD
W/ SHINGLE TRIM

10'-0" AWAY

24' MIN.

12
6

HIDDEN LINE DENOTES BOTTOM
CHORD OF SCISSOR TRUSS

TOP OF PLATE

36" HIGH GUARDRAILING

8'-0 3/4"

FINISHED FLOOR

ABOVE AND BELOW: A one-floor cabin is transformed into an Arts & Crafts–style bungalow by the use of a pergola, stone bases for column support, and natural siding material mixed for contrast and texture. The window grilles were changed from full size to a six-over-one pattern. The four-square window is a common Arts & Crafts detail. (BEFORE AND AFTER)

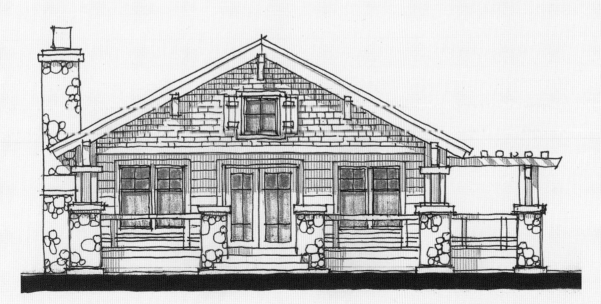

RIGHT AND ABOVE: The designer's artistry can transform a simple home into a structure with depth and personality. Simple things like an added porch pergola or cupola placed in the right spot with the perfect proportions can add to any home's design, turning average into spectacular. (BEFORE AND AFTER)

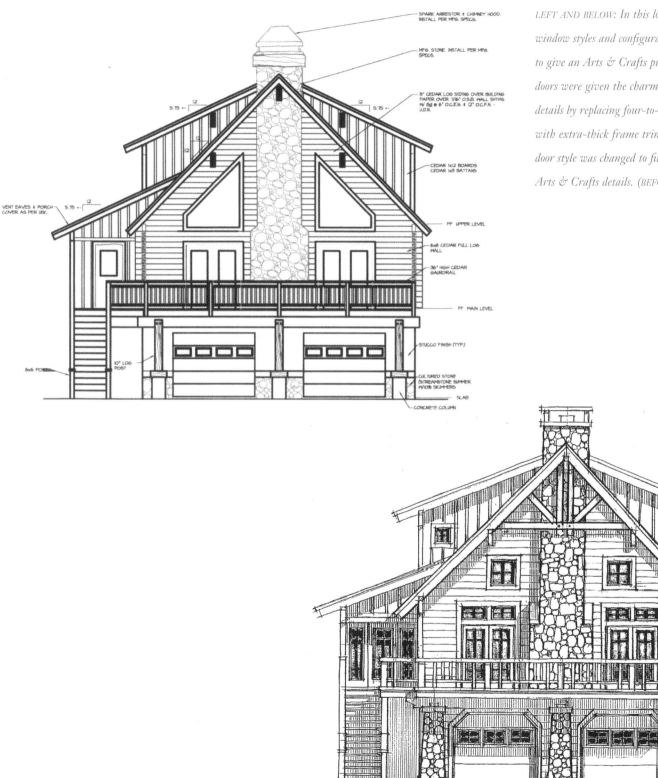

SPARK ARRESTOR & CHIMNEY HOOD. INSTALL PER MFG. SPECS.

MFG. STONE. INSTALL PER MFG. SPECS.

8" CEDAR LOG SIDING OVER BUILDING PAPER OVER 7/16" O.S.B. WALL SHTHG. W/ 8d @ 6" O.C.E.N. & 12" O.C.F.N. - U.O.N.

CEDAR 1x12 BOARDS & CEDAR 1x3 BATTANS

FF UPPER LEVEL

6x8 CEDAR FULL LOG WALL

36" HIGH CEDAR GAURDRAIL

FF MAIN LEVEL

5.75

12

5.75

12

12

5.75

12

12

VENT EAVES & PORCH COVER AS PER UBC.

6x6 POST

10" LOG POST

STUCCO FINISH (TYP)

CULTURED STONE (STREAMSTONE SUMMER W/1015 SKIMMERS

SLAB

CONCRETE COLUMN

LEFT AND BELOW: In this log home plan, the window styles and configurations were changed to give an Arts & Crafts punch. Windows and doors were given the charm of historic framing details by replacing four-to-six-inch boards with extra-thick frame trim. Even the garage-door style was changed to fit the home's new Arts & Crafts details. (BEFORE AND AFTER)

By microanalyzing the home's exterior, you can greatly improve its overall curb appeal with added drama, textures, rustic flavor, and storybook charm. It will also help you to be confident about the choices you make regarding design and the type of materials and accents you choose. And it will save you time later by not having to make last-minute changes on-site.

The Craftsman and Bungalow styles of architecture combined with timber joinery are age-old American traditions of which we can all be proud. In a day when there is so much confusion, shoddiness, and materialism, it is refreshing that many homeowners want to return to something simple and basic. The land will embrace you as you seek to bring nature and quality craftsmanship back into your home, creating happiness and harmony through a practical and more casual form of living.

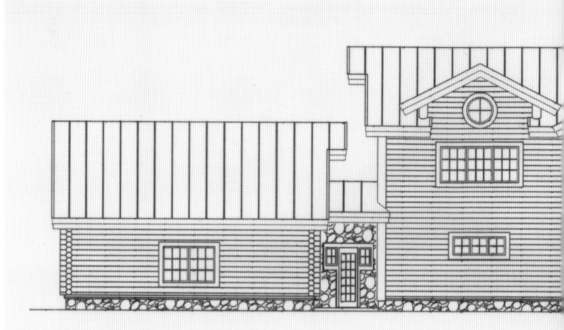

LEFT AND BELOW: The designer transformed this large log estate into an Arts & Crafts log-element structure. Log accents can be built with whole round logs (also shown on page 44) instead of square-cut timbers, depending on the look you are trying to achieve. (BEFORE AND AFTER)

Key Craftsman-Style Components

THE ARTS & CRAFTS STYLE OF CONSTRUCTION AND DESIGN HAS ALWAYS FEATURED AND HONORED COVERED PORCHES, SUNLIT PATIOS, AND SUN-DRENCHED TERRACES. LOG ELEMENTS SUCH AS RAFTERS AND TRUSSES ADD TO THE ARCHITECTURAL SPIRIT OF THE CLASSIC AMERICAN PORCH. THESE OUTDOOR LIVING ROOMS ARE RAPIDLY REGAINING POPULARITY.

SHELTERING PORCHES

Porches, decks, and patios are often overlooked and underestimated in the planning stage. Adding porches to a design can easily extend the living space and create a balance to the house and property. With smart exterior planning, most houses can gain an extra outdoor room that the family can enjoy in warm

OPPOSITE: This structure has simple lines and just a few timber elements. Shingle siding gives the home added strength and texture.

ABOVE: *Arched struts are not just decorative but serve a purpose in proper joinery of a post-and-beam structural element. These struts help keep a structure from "racking," or folding, to the left or right over time. This added "webbing" is key to a quality-built structure that will stand the test of time.*

RIGHT: *Shingles, clapboard, stone, and log elements add character to this home's exterior. The mix of these materials gives depth and texture to any home. The log porch columns are elevated off the ground by natural stone bases.*

weather. Not everyone is blessed with rolling lawns and expansive terraces. Even if you have a wooded lot or sloping terrain, don't let that stop you from creating an exciting and stylish outdoor room. Create a room where everyone wants to hang out. Every design detail counts toward ensuring that your outdoor living room becomes what you need.

The design and planning of a porch plays an important part in the home's feel, function, and overall flow. A porch in the right location can catch the summer breeze, soak up some sun rays, or capture nature's panoramic view. It is a perfect cool spot to sip lemonade on a sultry summer day or just the right place to enjoy a quiet cup of morning tea as you watch the mist dissipate into the rising sun.

OPPOSITE: *Porches have always been featured and honored within the design of an Arts & Crafts home. With new technologies, stains have been formulated specifically for whole-log and timber construction. These stains come in limitless color choices and have been specifically developed to penetrate deeper into the log's cell structure, allowing the log to breathe. Standard surface stains for furniture and milled wood are not the same. The use of these specialized stains can be crucial to the longevity of whole-log construction methods.*

ABOVE: *Outdoor rooms with romantic charm and classic details can be places where everyone gravitates.*

PORCH DESIGN AND DÉCOR—IDEAS

- An old barrel can be used for holding fishing poles and brooms or for storing winter salt.

- Use the log or timber roof rafters to mount a canoe, hang life jackets, or display or store other décor.

- Use an old trunk to store outdoor cushions or life jackets.

- A generous chest does double duty as a seating spot and storage space for all the gardening tools.

- Use older furniture, rugs, and standard interior décor items (such as candles, vases, knick-knacks, and curtains) to make the porch feel cozy.

- During warm weather, bring out your houseplants and set them around the deck to add some texture and life to your outdoor space. When houseplants are given a "summer break," the results of lush, overflowing foliage can be a winter reward.

- A porch swing can be enjoyed at any age. (But the porch swing does not have to be limited to the porch. Use a porch swing in a bathroom or kitchen for a touch of added fun and whimsy.)

- Outdoor curtains and roller shades can be adjusted on the porch to protect you from the glaring sun or chilling winds, or for additional privacy.

- Although we live in bug and black fly country, we usually do not enclose our porches with screens because we want a direct connection with the yard or water views. After living a while with open porches and ceiling fans (they really help to keep bugs at bay), many people find that in some situations the benefits of an open porch far outweigh any problems with insects, including the hassle of cleaning and fixing screens.

- Adding a porch may be economical compared to building a full solarium. With careful planning, you can design a covered porch with the intention of converting it into a closed-in solarium when your budget allows.

- To get ideas on what type of porch would best suit your home, be on the lookout. Take pictures, flag your design books, and collect clippings. A few good pictures can be worth a thousand words when trying to relay your ideas to a designer or builder.

STONE PATIOS AND TERRACES

An uncovered deck, terrace, or patio can really complement a home by imitating its architectural style and providing additional space for comfortable and cozy outdoor living. Although the standard wood deck is often a first choice, another nice backyard alternative is the more traditional stone terrace. Stone always improves with age and exposure to nature's elements. These stone hardscapes can be formal or informal, depending on the cut or texture of the natural stone. Stone paving classics are generally a more expensive option than a standard wood deck. However, a stone patio is more upscale and durable, which may be a good investment if you plan to stay in the home for a long period of time.

Proper installation is essential to obtaining the perfect patio. Although it is true that concrete, stone, and

brick stand the test of time better than wood, their worst enemy can also be water. Rain and snow can seep into their base where the cycles of freezing and thawing can crack concrete, stone, or brick if there is lack of proper drainage or improper installation. This continuing cycle can also

Adding an outdoor fireplace and spa can create a focal point for an outdoor room. Attention to detail, creativity, and a respect for nature can help seat the home's design into the landscape.

cause underground heaving, which creates an uneven surface. However, this is only likely to occur if the installation has been done improperly.

Exterior stone maintenance is generally minimal if it has been installed properly. The stonework can be either imbedded in concrete or laid directly into the ground without concrete. These are known respectively as "wet" and "dry" installations. I prefer the look of a dry installation because of the beautiful artistry created by traditional dry-lay methods and because it has a better capability for drainage if installed properly. Either way, to achieve a quality stone or brick patio requires additional thought and experience. For do-it-yourselfers, there are extensive how-to books on the market. Good construction trade magazines also provide informative step-by-step installation instructions.

INDOOR FIREPLACES

A fireplace is usually the center of attention; it creates the ambiance and mood that evokes a calming effect and has always been the focus of Craftsman- and Bungalow-style homes. Great thought and planning are given to the hearth's placement in the Arts & Crafts home. Inglenooks are a common design element that create an area where one can enjoy an inviting, luminous fire and take the chill off even the coldest winter nights. There is something undeniably soothing and romantic about watching the strobing colors of a fire's flames and listening to the crackling blaze with friends and family gathered around.

This is a more contemporary translation of the Craftsman- and Bungalow-style home, with massive whole-log columns and a central focus on the home's hearth.

The traditional romance of an open fire is perfect if you enjoy the ritual of cutting and stacking firewood. But if you prefer the instant magic of a switch to create a flame, then you'll probably want to spend some added time researching the newer gas units. However, if you are most concerned with using a more efficient heat source, then a wood or pellet stove may be your personal option. Many wood-burning stoves are designed solely to produce heat and, therefore, encase the fire's flame, which prevents visual enjoyment. The sealed firebox becomes less visible, but it consumes less fuel as it contains and radiates more heat within the structure.

A hand-hewn timber is used as a fireplace mantel to display handmade pottery and works of nature. The artistry of the mason is evident in the "dry stanch" style of stonework. The hand-hammered dimples of the iron create a depth of texture that complements the stonework.

This game room only has a hint of log work in the coffee table where large cants of squared timbers are mortised together with metal. Not all log-element homes have a lot of log details; there may not even be any log structural frame within a home. Some homes may only have log details in the railings; others may have a combination of trusses, stairs, rails, and floor joists. It is up to the homeowners and their designer to specify the log elements to be incorporated into the conventional construction.

ABOVE: Fireplaces are the center of importance in an Arts & Crafts home. The hearth was the family center of the late-nineteenth-century Arts & Crafts structure.

LEFT: This mantel is built with conventional boards and moldings that produce a formal outcome. The mix of iron and wood within the bed's footboard creates a sense of craftsmanship that is part of the Arts & Crafts tradition of working with talented craftspeople who can create any handmade item.

The fireplace mantel can be the added touch that accents a traditional hearth. The design possibilities are endless. Overscaled, massive, whole-log or square-beam mantels are fireside classics in a log-element structure. Keep in mind that a fireplace does not necessarily need a mantel to look good. Skillful carpentry or masonry that uses quality stone or brick patterns can be all that is needed to create an artful centerpiece.

RIGHT: Fireplaces are the center of importance in Arts & Crafts–style homes. This modern hearth's designer added a creative step with a large overhang that does double duty as a wood storage nook.

OPPOSITE: The attention to detail and use of texture is part of the Arts & Crafts influence and philosophy where craftsmanship is quality, not quantity.

FIREPLACE TIPS AND TECHNIQUES

- Cast-iron firebacks can be placed at the back of the fireplace to protect the masonry work while absorbing and radiating additional heat.

- A heat exchanger—which has the ability to transfer heat from the fireplace into hot water that is piped through the fireplace—can be installed. The resulting warm water circulates into a storage tank and can provide most of the home's hot water.

- A large ceiling fan can drive rising warm air back down into the room, keeping temperatures more even throughout the home.

- Flue enclosures and stonework can be shared by backing the two units against each other, thus reducing the cost of construction.

- Imposing fireplaces should not be placed in a way that will compete with scenic views.

- The romance and charm of a fireplace are what dreams are made of, but if your budget does not allow for one, direct your efforts and attention to other areas of the home to give it added character. All being said, some of the most charming homes do not have fireplaces.

OUTDOOR FIREPLACES

Building an outdoor fireplace is one of the most popular modern design fashions. An outdoor fireplace can make the garden area the most used part of the home. It should be easily accessible and connected to the main house in some way—by walks or a connecting terrace. A dining or sitting area will give this featured spot added function and purpose that will invariably lead to more use.

Playing a game of cards, roasting marshmallows under the stars, or cooking hot dogs over an open flame transforms an ordinary event into an extraordinary memory. The outdoor fireplace can also give an adventurous cook the opportunity to try a hand at preparing creative meals over an open flame.

OPPOSITE: The open walls of glass capture water views, while the use of overhead transoms capture the sky.

WINDOWSCAPES

Windows have always been an important part of any home. In an Arts & Crafts home, they are even more of a focus because of added health benefits as well as the overall design concept of the home's connection to the outdoors. Arts & Crafts windows are defined by the philosophy of simplicity and allow a great deal of sunlight and fresh air into the home. Large windows, windows with stacked transoms, windows with eyebrow arches, or a series of square windows with grilles of different patterns can all be used to the home's advantage. Many Arts & Crafts–style windows were borrowed from the traditional window patterns to portray a cottage or bungalow feel. The perfect combination of windows can add a nice touch to an otherwise simple home appearance.

LEFT: The use of carefully designed and placed windows brings nature indoors, capturing the mood of the outdoors.

ABOVE: The design professional mimicked the arch of the trusses with the use of a combination of windows. The timber-frame joinery may look like simple connections, but years of experience is required to achieve this level of joinery.

PREVIOUS PAGE: *A circular wall of windows adds a light-filled dining area that gives the sense of plenty of extra space without constructing another room.*

ABOVE: *A wall of windows captures the great view while allowing plenty of light into the kitchen. An added outdoor patio creates dining and lounging space.*

LEFT: Oversized timbers are doubled on the base collar tie to add interest as well as extra strength to the ceiling of this spacious living area. The materials you select will dictate what application can or should be used for your log home. Check with your log builder or design professional.

In all homes, the balance and placement of windows is very important, as windows distinguish the character of the dwelling. A house can be cast out of proportion and money may be wasted when too many or too few windows are installed. On the other hand, a window in just the right place can take advantage of natural light and extend a room's size, opening the interior rooms to the outside world. The use of windows to frame nature is a wonderful design advantage, especially if there is a great outdoor view. Windows can create an airy, light-filled room and make a boring, bland space come to life.

In planning and designing a home, consider the window's base height. The window could possibly be moved closer to ground level in a bedroom, living room, or dining area. In these settings, windows can properly capture the outside landscape and create a better view of nature's theater while the occupants rest in bed, sit at the table, or curl up on the sofa. Careful placement and choice of windows can enhance even the simplest and modest home.

Windows can be works of art in themselves. Study the various windows available and decide which ones will best reflect your own personal philosophy for your home.

A mix of contemporary Arts & Crafts furnishings is used to accent the room. Walls of windows usher the light indoors.

LEFT: *Mission-style accents and vaulted ceilings give this room an inviting feel. The stained-glass door is another charming detail.*

OPPOSITE: *Windows with overhead transoms capture open views and starlit nights.*

RIGHT: Any cat would love a cozy loft to relax in, view the home's activity, and just soak up the day's sun.

BELOW: Quarter-sawn oak sideboards and Mission-style table and chairs radiate a warm glow from wood surfaces.

OPPOSITE: *Hammer-beam trusses are exposed structural elements. Here they are further highlighted by a combination of arched top windows accentuating nature's theater beyond.*

LEFT: *Wide-board, slat-back chairs are cut to showcase the natural oak grain (see page 25 for an explanation of quarter-sawn oak).*

ABOVE: *A mix of wood handrails and shoe rails cap the iron spindles. The heavy materials create a sense of permanence and stability in this structure.*

OPPOSITE: *Stone columns flank the stove unit and are topped with a row of oversized wood moldings, a signature of this design professional. Overhead skylights add some natural light to the kitchen.*

BUILT-IN DETAILS

The smaller footprint of the Arts & Crafts home led builders to create efficient use of every space available. Therefore, these homes are known for their built-in units of sideboards, hutches, drawers, shelves, breakfast nooks, seating alcoves, or under-the-stairs built-in units. Arts & Crafts homes also feature other types of storage that make the best of otherwise unusable space or that sensibly utilize the limited available space.

It is to your advantage to plan for built-in spaces in the early stages of a home's design to allow more flexibility and to ensure that the built-in does not detract from the overall design of the home. Other clever initiatives are to

create a built-in bunk or a bed with privacy curtains, cut a dresser out of a sloping kneewall (the short wall left where the intersection of wall and sloping roofline meet), or divide a long, boring wall or an awkward nook with a desk or armoire. A well-designed built-in unit results in a room that feels and looks more spacious.

With careful consideration, one can maximize the use of the most unusual areas while creating effective and aesthetically pleasing design solutions. The more awkward areas—such as the low headroom of a kneewall, the space under the stairs, small nooks, shared spaces, and

LEFT: Today's modern electronics (like this built-in television) are combined with a more traditional hearth. A built-in window seat captures the panoramic views and becomes a cozy place to curl up and read a book by the warmth of the fire.

NEXT PAGE: A large-cut slab of wood is used as a breakfast bar. The higher bar ledge can help hide the mess of the lower counter's clutter. Note the use of four-over-one windows with wide mullions.

LEFT: *Built-in seating areas are part of the Arts & Crafts–design detailing. This more contemporary form of clean-line benches with lavender-accented wall is a modern translation of the Arts & Crafts influence. The contemporary colors are a contrast to the softness of the wood truss and knotty-pine ceiling boards.*

OPPOSITE: *Textured stone and the warmth of wood and hammered metals create depth within the stairway hall. These elements are classic details of Arts & Crafts Prairie-style homes.*

BELOW: *The composition on the front of this small cubicle creates an interesting design detail.*

niches—can enrich a home once you discover how to best use the space in these often-wasted areas. It can be fun to research deeper into your "design pockets" to create more practical storage solutions and to realize how workplaces and other rooms can serve a variety of purposes. Having a comfortable and efficient home work space is part of today's trend toward utilitarian design; it is no longer considered a luxury.

OPPOSITE: *A whole wall of built-in cabinetry makes for plenty of added storage.*

RIGHT: *These built-in dining benches echo traditional bungalow dining nooks while utilizing the natural beauty of wood.*

LEFT: *The dark tone of the wood cabinets are a great contrast to the white walls and ceilings. In the sunroom, a wood ceiling is used to balance the overall tone and abundance of light.*

ABOVE: *A contemporary influence of Arts & Crafts–style design is used on this home's entry. Oversized whole round logs stand like soldiers guarding the gate. Note the skylight above the entry.*

OPPOSITE: *Pure geometry is the focus of this home's stair design. Open stair risers create an airy feel to the entry.*

LEFT: *Between the large, square columns the designer made use of the otherwise wasted space.*

LEFT: *Built-in nooks add to the romance of the Craftsman- and Bungalow-style home. The bar is perfect for entertaining.*

OPPOSITE: *Color is used in contrast to the subtle tone of the natural wood for a more modern form of décor.*

RIGHT: *Timber-frame joints are filled in with a gridwork pattern on the ceiling to add architectural interest.*

The look of built-ins can be quaint and charming, adding character to an area otherwise devoid of architectural interest. With good craftsmanship, sophisticated joinery, and high-quality wood, one can set the overall tone and feel of a structure with its built-in furniture units. Every household can use more storage space that is easily accessible. The storage space should hold a wide variety of items, be practical, and flexible. You will find that when you have fashioned these areas, you will have reduced stress and created more time to enjoy life. When every inch of the home is properly evaluated for flow and function, the end result will be less clutter and less wasted space.

A light-filled area is immersed in nature with accents of twig antlers and a base of bright color. A built-in wet bar features an area for convenient entertainment.

OPPOSITE: *Contemporary architecture is influenced by Arts & Crafts design principles. The exposed cables are not just decorative but also structural components. The railings are designed with horizontal cables that mimic the truss cables.*

ABOVE: *Arts & Crafts–style lighting is suspended above the kitchen's center island, casting a soft glow to the area.*

OPPOSITE: *Iron and wood are a complementary mix of contrasting materials typical of Craftsman- and Bungalow-style homes.*

LEFT: *This home has an eclectic mix of styles with only a hint of Arts & Crafts style in the stairs and window combinations.*

ABOVE: *The vibrant warmth of wood, the strength of stone, the contrast of wrought iron, and the delicate artistry of stained glass are the combined elements that become the central base components of Craftsman- or Bungalow-style architecture.*

OPPOSITE: *The changing slope of the intersecting rooflines offers added interest and drama.*

RIGHT: *A craftsman-built door creates the look of a solid fortress. Open risers within the stairs give a sense of openness.*

BUILT-IN SPACE-SAVING IDEAS

- The dead space in the wall cavity, such as the shower area, can be used to create shelves for shampoos, soaps, and sponges.

- A wall cavity in the kitchen area can be fashioned into a spice rack.

- In the bathroom next to the water closet, the wall cavity can be utilized for a built-in magazine rack or bathroom tissue holder.

- A ceiling cavity can be developed to house a retractable home-theater projection screen.

- With a traditional fireplace taking center stage, a modern problem is where to position the television. A built-in television console can be designed right in the fireplace wall or built in to flank the fire unit.

- A Murphy bed (a bed that folds up into the wall or furniture unit) can be built into a wall unit or a small niche in a wall.

- A window seat can be made into a cozy breakfast nook, a bedroom reading alcove, a great phone "gossip" bench, or an extra living room sofa. It could also serve as a reading sanctuary in the library or as a miniature indoor greenhouse.

- The kneewall slope of the roof system can be used as space for a front-loading washer and dryer; an area for storing unused seasonal décor items, seasonal clothes, luggage, and mechanical odds and ends; a spot to feature bookshelves and dressers; or as a central vacuum system center.

- A built-in playhouse can be carved out of the often-wasted space under the stairs. This unusual area can also be transformed into a juice bar or an efficient kitchenette.

- With a high vaulted ceiling, a room can accommodate an added bunk loft with ladder, perfect for additional sleeping space for grandchildren or the young at heart.

- The bump-outs of an added dormer can create a great space for a soaking tub in the bathroom or bedroom, a naturally lit built-in vanity, an inspirational desk nook, or a unique window seat high among the treetops.

OPPOSITE: Today's central "hearth" in a home tends to be the television. With creative design and careful planning, there can be unique solutions to disguising it.

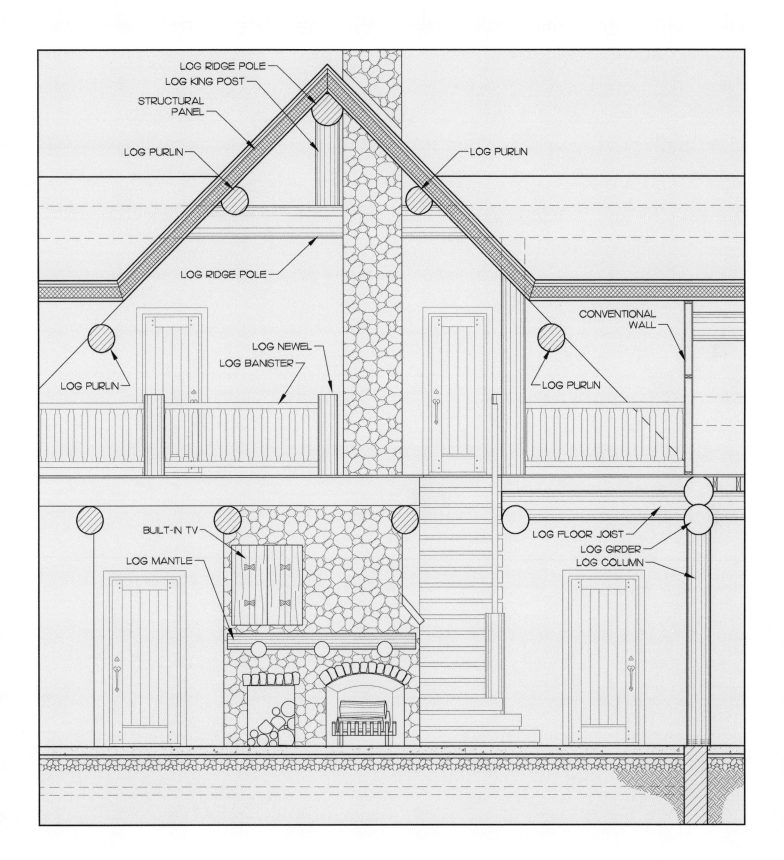

LOG RIDGE POLE

LOG KING POST

STRUCTURAL PANEL

LOG PURLIN

LOG PURLIN

LOG RIDGE POLE

CONVENTIONAL WALL

LOG NEWEL

LOG BANISTER

LOG PURLIN

LOG PURLIN

BUILT-IN TV

LOG FLOOR JOIST

LOG GIRDER

LOG COLUMN

LOG MANTLE

Unused space beneath the slope of the stairs can be transformed into usable storage or display areas.

LEFT: The windows in this bathroom are placed low enough to soak in the views.

ABOVE: *An odd corner is transformed into a room with character. The offset log timber adds even more architectural interest to this home's bathroom. Note how the lights above the sink "grow" out of the mirror. These are design touches that add personality and whimsy to a home's design.*

RIGHT: *Here built-in bunks add two beds to the limited amount of space while keeping much of the room as open as possible. Even the bump-out window makes use of every available inch.*

RIGHT: *Carved-out niches can create better use of space within a smaller footprint. Quality over quantity is the Arts & Crafts philosophy.*

OPPOSITE: *A corner niche becomes a showplace by a perfectly chosen piece of furniture. The built-in bookcase and light fixtures are nice examples of Arts & Crafts style.*

An extra sleeping area carved out of a hallway nook makes the most
of a tight and narrow space with plenty of closets and storage.

OPPOSITE: *A soaking tub is tucked into a niche. The combination of wood, tile,
and light make a calm setting for a pleasurable in-home spa treatment.*

ABOVE: *Massive, whole-log outrigger beams are the perfect contrast to the square upright grouping of log columns and decorative grid-work lattice that closes up the gable end. This is truly an outdoor room for relaxation with views of pure inspiration.*

OPPOSITE: *The log builder and designer of this home captured the Arts & Crafts influence and Adirondack flair that is still popular in today's home designs. This hybrid form of log architecture combined with Arts & Crafts details offers hints of the Adirondacks no matter where the home is located.*

TRUSSES

In a traditional Craftsman or Bungalow home, the use of trusses was somewhat understated or not at all part of the design. Today's hybrid log and timber trusses are featured to add a craftsman's touch to an otherwise simple design. Traditional handcrafted timber elements provide a classic look and feel, but many new hybrids of whole-log elements can be added to create a new twist of whole-log accents.

Each raw log has its own presence and character that can add substance to a home's design. The architectural signature of a handcrafted truss can bring drama to almost any style of

BELOW: *Hand-hewn, oversized collar ties are tripled and supported by full-round log timber columns. This combination of round-on-round and square-intersecting-round log joinery is part of the new hybrid in log-element construction methods.*

OPPOSITE: *This general form of construction is the typical hybrid style of joinery of log-element architecture. This home is built using round log columns that lead up to massive, triple-stacked purlins that support the weight of the roof and snow load. Also, notice how logs are used for trim molding. The large stone columns help balance the visual weight of the log timbers.*

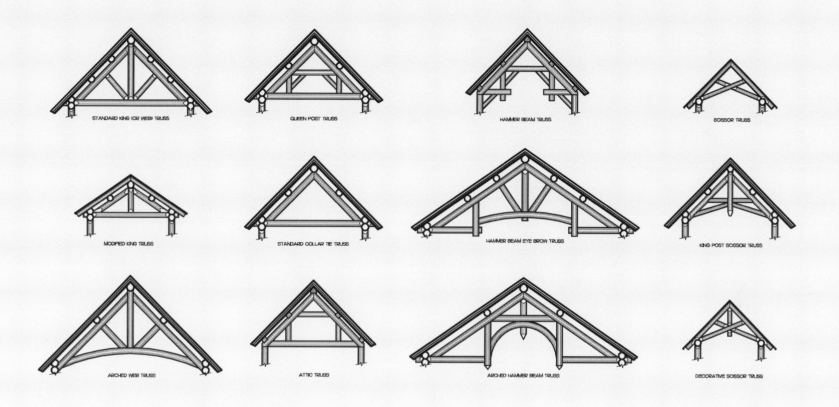

STANDARD KING (OR WEB) TRUSS   QUEEN POST TRUSS   HAMMER BEAM TRUSS   SCISSOR TRUSS

MODIFIED KING TRUSS   STANDARD COLLAR TIE TRUSS   HAMMER BEAM EYE BROW TRUSS   KING POST SCISSOR TRUSS

ARCHED WEB TRUSS   ATTIC TRUSS   ARCHED HAMMER BEAM TRUSS   DECORATIVE SCISSOR TRUSS

ABOVE: These are a few common styles of Arts & Crafts–influenced truss combinations. Some are traditional styles while others are modern hybrid styles. Some of the truss designs are more structural than others; truss designs must be carefully considered in their placement and use. The trusses can be built in all-square connections, or all-round connections, or a combination of both square and round.

OPPOSITE: The new hybrid of log-element construction is known for its full-round log work left within its natural form. The round-on-round style of connection is a great contrast to the flat surfaces of conventional construction.

structure. There are so many styles of trusses and design possibilities that you are limited only by your imagination. The following pages show some examples of log truss styles that can enhance your Craftsman home. The trusses can be made of squared timbers, full-round logs, or a combination of both round and square. Round-on-round (whole- or full-log) joinery will create a very different architectural appearance than a square timber-frame truss system. (See example on page 44 for round-on-round log style of connections of trusses.)

ABOVE: *Handcrafted square-timber trusses are supported by full-round log columns that, with the craftsman's skills, appear to grow out of one another. The arched door and continuous sidelights are accentuated by the added use of arched timber trusses.*

RIGHT: *This is a classic example of just one of many styles of log-element hybrid details where oversized square-log beams intersect full-round log ridgepoles and purlins, creating a drive-through portico. Log elements can add drama and presence to any structure when a skilled designer, experienced log craftsperson, and general contractor work together, contributing their individual talents.*

OPPOSITE: *The Adirondack influence combined with Arts & Crafts details has a fluid feel that blends with nature.*

ABOVE: *Hammer-beam truss combinations are a tradition of log-timber joinery still kept alive by modern-day craftsmen. Square-timber joinery methods are a very old form of construction. Some methods are used in a more traditional form of post-and-beam construction and others are used in a hybrid form where there is no longer a full frame or skeleton of log work, only elements or "bits and pieces" used with a conventionally built frame (see example on page 132).*

LEFT: *The ceiling's gridwork of log timbers creates architectural interest. The English-style grille pattern on the door echoes the ceiling.*

ABOVE: *A Mission-style padded bench is a place to sit and view the handcrafted timber trusses and intersecting purlins that span from truss to truss.*

OPPOSITE: *The intersection of knee braces and timber struts incorporates nature into the home's design. The skill of knowing each wood species and its capabilities is learned over years of training, allowing a handcraft timber-framer and log-builder to make the best choice of material for the application within the structure. This practical experience is where the art of log joinery is brought to a whole new level of craftsmanship.*

OPPOSITE: *Heavy timber vaulted ceilings are set off with a high dividing wall creatively topped with a completely round log. The very crooked log is artfully used to cap the lower dividing wall while leaving the log work within the ceiling fully exposed.*

ABOVE: *Extended outrigger beams are supported by knee braces. These architectural details bring added interest to this home's entry. The outrigger extensions could have copper "saddles" made to greatly extend the life of the log outrigger beams exposed to nature's elements.*

CREATING HANDCRAFTED LOG ELEMENTS

It is easy to see the care and sensitivity that go into each and every log cut of well-crafted log work. Discipline, hard work, and an appreciation for natural materials are the life of a log craftsman. To work in harmony with nature, one must be able to accept the natural imperfections of raw materials and learn ways to work with them.

Mastering the world of handcrafted log building demands patience and dedication. The log builder often possesses a resourceful nature and way of life that involves constant sacrifices. Many of the materials used are raw, organic substances that command a reverence and respect. Logs are living, breathing elements with natural dynamics and properties that are not familiar to most people today.

Log-building and timber-framing techniques are a centuries-old tradition that primarily utilizes handheld tools such as axes, chisels, and scribers. These standard tools and methods have not changed over hundreds of years, although some power-assisted tools—such as chain saws, electric sanders, and heavy equipment for moving full-length logs—have been added to help speed up this time-consuming form of construction. Each log is meticulously cut and shaped for one specific location in the structure, which is primarily assembled in the log craftsperson's compound.

Although rustic in nature, today's log-hybrid elements are far from unsophisticated. Many of the tools still used in the construction of a handcrafted log and timber structure are quite medieval in appearance and may seem primitive in this high-tech era. This slow and traditional method of construction is still the best way to build handcrafted log-element structures. Each hand-peeled component of a whole-log structure is meticulously scribed and pieced together like a jigsaw puzzle to achieve a sculptured fit.

The modern-day masters of handcrafted log construction are preserving a tradition that was nearly lost, ensuring that this unique legacy can continue for generations to come.

OPPOSITE: *The clean lines of this home office give an uncluttered place to work, while the views to nature bring in the tranquility of the outdoors. The matching grille pattern on the French doors and windows tie the room together.*

LEFT: The rhythm of timber rafters extend far past the home's walls, creating not only protection for the siding but also an added cover above the entry.

ABOVE: Closely set ceiling joints run the opposite way of the kitchen cabinetry, creating texture and visual interest.

ABOVE: *The kitchen windows are the four-pane square style that are very common in Arts & Crafts–style homes. Note how the carpenters extended the base of the windowsill for a deep ledge to place plants and décor items.*

OPPOSITE: *The living room vaults two stories with a hammer-beam truss overhead. Notice that the truss behind the hammer-beam truss is a simple king-post truss, or A-truss. The trusses do not have to be the same style to work well with one another.*

OPPOSITE: *A small, intimate table is showered with light from a large set of windows with an English grille pattern.*

RIGHT: *Composing furnishings and structural elements into an orchestrated elegant interpretation of nature is a primary goal of Arts & Crafts architecture.*

Working with Design Professionals

Handcrafted trusses are truly limitless in possibilities of design combinations. Employing the experience of the log builder/timber framer and design professional is the only way to create classic, well-built handcrafted homes. This is where years of experience and practical knowledge are paramount to the home's outcome and level of artistry.

ORKING WITH A DESIGN PROFESSIONAL SHOULD NOT BE DIFFICULT. IT IS A STEP-BY-STEP PROCESS THAT YOUR DESIGNER WILL PROMPT YOU THROUGH. NEVERTHELESS, YOU MUST FIRST KNOW AND UNDERSTAND YOUR GENERAL LIKES AND DISLIKES. HAVING A LIST OF NEEDS VS. WISHES AND COLLECTING PHOTOS OF WHAT REALLY APPEALS TO YOU WILL HELP TREMENDOUSLY TO FIND THE TRUE BASE OF YOUR FAMILY REQUIREMENTS AND DESIGN TASTES.

DESIGN PROCESS FLOWCHART

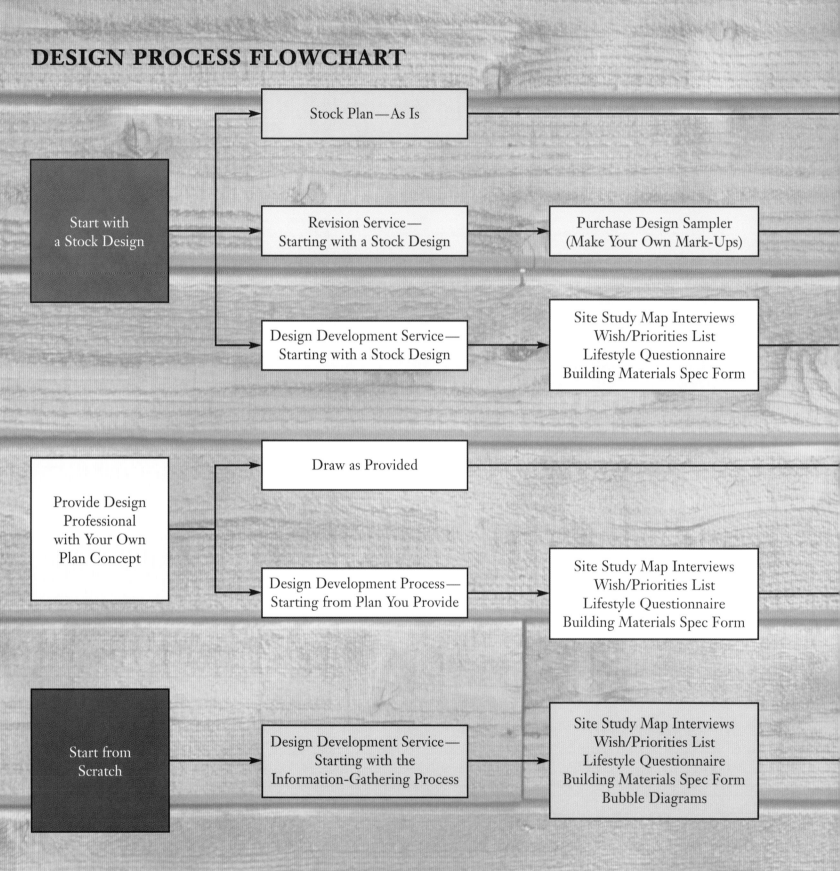

Start with a Stock Design

Stock Plan—As Is

Revision Service—
Starting with a Stock Design

Purchase Design Sampler
(Make Your Own Mark-Ups)

Design Development Service—
Starting with a Stock Design

Site Study Map Interviews
Wish/Priorities List
Lifestyle Questionnaire
Building Materials Spec Form

Provide Design
Professional
with Your Own
Plan Concept

Draw as Provided

Design Development Process—
Starting from Plan You Provide

Site Study Map Interviews
Wish/Priorities List
Lifestyle Questionnaire
Building Materials Spec Form

Start from
Scratch

Design Development Service—
Starting with the
Information-Gathering Process

Site Study Map Interviews
Wish/Priorities List
Lifestyle Questionnaire
Building Materials Spec Form
Bubble Diagrams

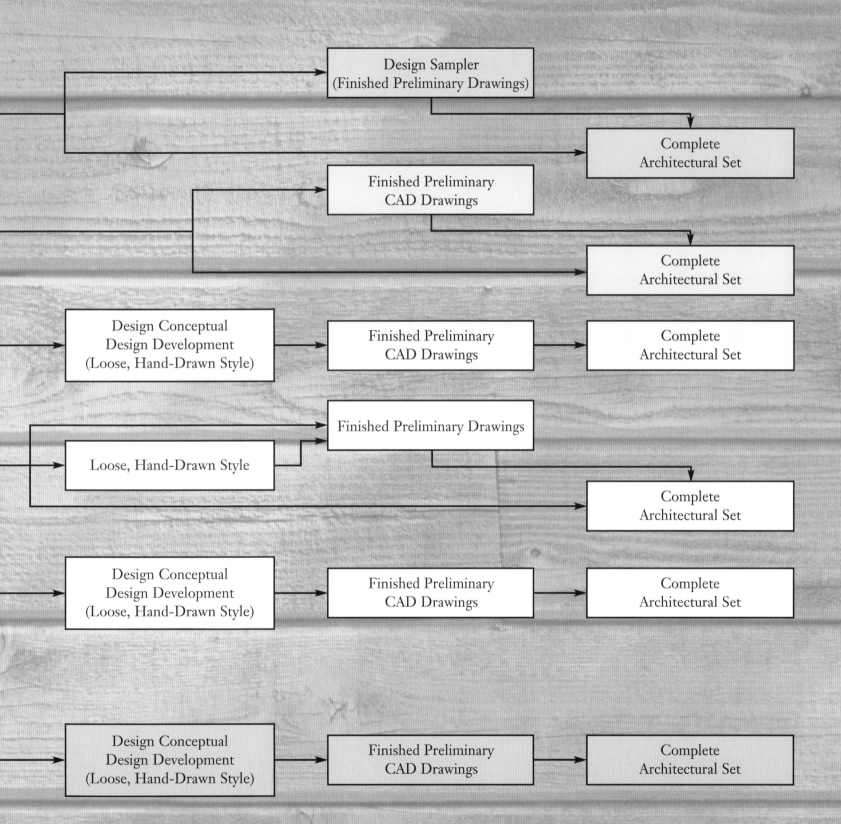

Design Sampler
(Finished Preliminary Drawings)

Complete
Architectural Set

Finished Preliminary
CAD Drawings

Complete
Architectural Set

Design Conceptual
Design Development
(Loose, Hand-Drawn Style)

Finished Preliminary
CAD Drawings

Complete
Architectural Set

Finished Preliminary Drawings

Loose, Hand-Drawn Style

Complete
Architectural Set

Design Conceptual
Design Development
(Loose, Hand-Drawn Style)

Finished Preliminary
CAD Drawings

Complete
Architectural Set

Design Conceptual
Design Development
(Loose, Hand-Drawn Style)

Finished Preliminary
CAD Drawings

Complete
Architectural Set

NOTE: Complete Construction Documents Follow the Above Process

© 2003 Alpenglow Mountain Home Designs

Over many years of consulting and viewing homes all over North America, I have learned that the construction projects that have used design professionals, or carefully and meticulously drawn plans, are more likely to be better constructed. They also have a more fluid use of space. It is very important to find a design

Walls of windows and doors with overhead transoms allow light to envelop all rooms. Note the curved railing on the lower right of the photo; with an Arts & Crafts–influenced spindle pattern that draws the eye.

professional who has a style that is close to your tastes and interests. With faxes and e-mail, it is very easy to work with a designer who does not live close to you. It's most important that your personalities and interests are similar. You must work with the design professional over months at a time, so the honeymoon can wear off quickly. If you do not seem to have a certain amount of chemistry with the people you are working with at the beginning, it does not get better as time goes on.

RIGHT: Log or timber collar ties and added struts are not just decorative but also very important structural elements that add long-term strength and durability to a home's design. It is important to find an experienced timber craftsman and design professional who understand the natural properties of log-element joinery.

BELOW: Using hand-hammered metals mixed with the warmth of wood is a design classic that transcends time. The ceiling's grid work of traditional handcrafted timbers adds visual interest to this master suite.

The maze of overhead log work

creates a grid system where the log's sheer mass

and dimension envelop all who enter.

OPPOSITE: *Much design time is required in any home, let alone a log or timber-frame structure, where the intersection of log elements and the home's décor become even more crucial. Here the design professional fluidly wrapped the kitchen counter around log timbers and used the support columns and overhead supporting girder as a natural dividing point.*

BELOW: *The placement of the windows is so important in a bedroom. Here the windows are low enough to let you enjoy the view while in bed.*

Construction plans and designs are a large part of the contract with your builder and subtrades. Be sure to get your ideas and thoughts on paper so that your needs and wishes become clear and visible for all the trades to understand. I see so many people build a home without clear direction and no formal drawings because they feel that drawings cost too much, but drawings are only a small part of the overall project. Blueprints are the only way to truly get close to the cost of actual construction. If you want an inexpensive way to price or design a home, then try finding a company that has a reputation for well-developed stock plans. If you find a stock plan that is similar to what you want, it is very cost-effective to customize the stock plan and have it fit within your needs at a fraction of the cost of a custom home plan.

The interesting grid pattern of the timber-frame work is used in a playful pattern and adds additional support and structural value to the home's design.

ABOVE: *Bead board cabinets and backsplashes are used along with Mission-style chairs. Note the grille pattern in the windows topped with a wide shelf above, perfect for added décor.*

LEFT: *Built-in cabinetry houses a set of sinks. In the sitting area beyond, there is an Arts & Crafts–style floor lamp with mica shade. The mica is a stone composite that is heated to just the right temperature, then slumped into the form of the mold to create its curved shape. Mica lampshades cast a very soft glow.*

Bead board cabinetry is contrasted by an island with a grid base. This very angular pattern is contrasted by the sweeping radius countertop that extends over the cabinets to create a breakfast bar.

Do not underestimate the power of good design. Careful planning and attention to details will enhance your home and increase its value. There is also the importance of curb appeal as well as the flow of a home's layout. These things can bring a higher level of sophistication to the project. But the most important service a design provides is to supply meaningful information that will help make the log-builder's and contractor's time on-site more productive.

Oversized accents and furnishings are important in log and timber-frame homes. If average in size, the massiveness of the logs or timber can feel out of scale.

RESOURCES

Professional Design Services Specializing in Whole-Log and/or Timber-Frame Methods

We have included design professionals who specialize in the Arts & Crafts form of construction and/or whole-log construction methods. These experienced design professionals will be able to help you capture your family's needs and dreams on paper so that all the trades involved will have the same point of direction.

BC MOUNTAIN HOMES
3444 Dunbar Street
Vancouver, BC v6s 2c2
www.BCmountainhomes.com
⊞ 877.366.2502

BEAVER CREEK CONSTRUCTION SERVICES
35 Territory Road
Oneida, NY 13483
www.beavercreekloghomes.com
⊞ 315.245.4112

THE BUNGALOW COMPANY
PO Box 584
Bend, OR 97709
www.thebungalowcompany.com
⊞ 888.945.9206

HOYLE, DORAN & BERRY, ARCHITECTS
83 Newbury Street
Boston, MA 02116
www.hdb.com
⊞ 617.424.6200

JEAN STEINBRECHER ARCHITECTS
PO Box 788
Langley, WA 98260
jsa@whidbey.com
⊞ 360.221.0494

JOHN MORRIS ARCHITECTS
31 Chestnut Street
Camden, ME 04843
www.johnmorrisarchitects.com
⊞ 207.236.8321

MOUNTAIN HOME DESIGNS.COM
Marty Wheeler
20 North Canyon Way
Colfax, CA 95713
www.mountainhomedesigns.com
⊞ 530.346.9999

Home designs featured within this book are for sale through Mountain Home Designs.Com. Design samplers or prelims can be purchased, and design development services and/or site-specific construction documentation can be commissioned based upon these or customer's alternate designs.

Established, Longtime Handcrafted Log Builders Specializing in Log-Element Building Methods

ACKERMAN HANDCRAFTED LOG HOMES
PO Box 1318
Carbondale, CO 81623
www.ackermanloghomes.com
⊞ 970.963.0119

ALPENGLOW LOG & TIMBER HOMES
Design Center and Log Yard
Marty Wheeler
20 North Canyon Way
Colfax, CA 95713
marty@alpenglow.com
logaccents.biz
⊞ 530.346.9999

Components and home packages for the home designs featured within this book are available, including engineered lumber; prefabricated SIP panels; wall logs; log accents; custom-milled beams, siding, and T&G patterns; windows; skylights; and more. Owner-builder consulting services and project management is also available in some regions.

BEAVER CREEK LOG HOMES
35 Territory Road
Oneida, NY 13483
www.beavercreekloghomes.com
☒ 315.245.4112

CUSTOM LOG HOMES
PO Box 218
3662 Highway 93 North
Stevensville, MT 59870
www.customlog.com
☒ 406.777.5202

HILGUARD LOG BUILDERS
PO Box 891
West Yellowstone, MT 59758
☒ 406.646.7234

**JOHN DEVRIES LOG
& TIMBER HOMES**
RR 3
Tweed, ON KOK 3JO
www.jdvloghomes.com
☒ 613.478.6830

MAPLE ISLAND LOG HOMES
5046 SW Bayshore Drive, Suite A
Suttons Bay, MI 49682
www.mapleisland.com
☒ 800.748.0137

**MINDE LOG
CONSTRUCTION INC.**
2112 East Pioneer Road
Duluth, MN 55806
www.mindelog.com
☒ 218.525.1070

OLD STYLE LOG WORKS INC.
PO Box 255
Kalispell, MT 59903
www.oldstylelogworks.com
☒ 888.850.4665

PEDERSEN LOGSMITHS, INC.
PO Box 788
Highway 93 North
Challis, ID 83226
www.pedersenlogsmiths.com
☒ 208.879.4211

THE WOODEN HOUSE CO.
3714 North Road
South Ryegate, VT 05069
☒ 802.429.2490

TIMMERHUS INC.
3105 North 75th Street
Boulder, CO 80301
www.timmerhusinc.com
☒ 303.449.1336

Handcrafted Log Builders Seldom Listed in the General Log-Building Publications

**INTERNATIONAL LOG
BUILDERS' ASSOCIATION**
PO Box 775
Lumby, BC VOE 2GO
www.logassociation.org
☒ 250.547.8776
☒ 800.532.2900

*The International Log Builders'
Association is one of the best-kept secrets of*

*listings for traditional handcrafted log
builders from around the world. These
names are the trade's top professionals who
do not often advertise within magazines
or trade-related magazines. The Log
Builders' Association has a large list of
members from all over the world that can
be obtained through its Web site, or you
may call their office for the members list.*

LOG HOME GUIDE
PO Box 671
1107 NW 4th Street
Grand Rapids, MN 55744
www.loghomeguide.com
☒ 888.345.LOGS [5647]

*Log Home Guide has a special-issue
magazine with a hand-selected list of the
top 100 log builders in North America,
a valuable resource list with company
information about handcrafted log
builders within your region and around
the world. This list has been collected by
invitation only, not by paid advertising.*

THE TIMBER-FRAMERS GUILD
PO Box 60
Becket, MA 01223
www.tfguild.org
☒ 888.453.0879

BOOKS FOR FURTHER RESEARCH:

THE NOT SO LOG CABIN
by Robbin Obomsawin

The new hybrid forms of handcrafted log construction within three distinctive regional architectural styles are featured here: Cowboy chic, Adirondack classics, and Southwest-style. The book illustrates how log elements can be effectively incorporated within home interiors and exteriors for added architectural punch. The book also has twenty-five floor plans as a base for log-element classics.

Gibbs Smith, Publisher
$39.95 U.S.
ISBN 1-58685-152-7
☒ 800.748.5439

LOG CONSTRUCTION MANUAL: THE ULTIMATE GUIDE TO BUILDING HANDCRAFTED LOG HOMES
by Robert W. Chambers

Here is knowledgeable, clear, and direct information to make it easier for new log builders to have meaningful and dependable guidelines for handcrafted log-building construction methods. This book is my pick for the person who is interested in more information and the technical aspects of log building, whole-log construction joinery methods, and log-construction tips. This is the information you should know and understand before you attempt to build a log home yourself. It is also the most important reference tool for experienced, handcrafted log builders.

Deep Stream Press
Distributed by Chelsea Green Publishing Company
$32.00 U.S.
ISBN 0-9715736-0-3
☒ 800.639.4099

THE BEAUTIFUL NECESSITY: DECORATING WITH ARTS & CRAFTS
by Bruce Smith and Yoshiko Yamamoto

The book goes into depth on some of the innovative minds of design and architecture within the Arts & Crafts movement, giving a cross-section of the elements that create an Arts & Crafts home, including wall coverings, furnishings, tiles, stenciling, accessories, moldings, and floor coverings. Styles from the East and West Coast as well as European and Japanese influences are discussed. It is everything you want to know about Arts & Crafts details and the people who influenced the Arts & Crafts movement. There is a nicely compiled list of Arts & Crafts resources as well.

Gibbs Smith, Publisher
$ 19.95 U.S., PAPERBACK
ISBN 1-58685-431-3
☒ 800.748.5439

BUNGALOW PLANS
by Christian and Christen Gladu

Twenty-five bungalow plans from the field's top designers are showcased. The homes featured illustrate how designers, homeowners, and builders have reinterpreted the bungalow philosophy for a new generation.

Gibbs Smith, Publisher
$24.95 U.S.
ISBN 1-58685-147-0
☒ 800.748.5439

BUNGALOW COLORS: EXTERIORS
by Robert Schweitzer

Read about the pallets of colors once used within Bungalow exteriors and address the importance of color in Arts & Crafts architecture. The author gives practical advice for those who wish to integrate historically accurate colors into their homes, whether restoring an older bungalow or aiming to impart a more authentic flavor to a new Arts & Crafts–style home.

Gibbs Smith, Publisher
$29.95 U.S.
ISBN 1-58685-130-6
▣ 800.748.5439

GREENE & GREENE: THE PASSION AND THE LEGACY
by Randell L. Makinson

The building history of brothers Henry and Charles Greene is written with a dedication and passion for the Greenes' influence on design. The author has clearly studied and compiled information that illustrates the architectural evolution of the Greene brothers' metamorphosis of architectural style and their influence on the Arts & Crafts movement of the early 1900s. It is an informative book with

a mix of old and new photographs, the Greenes' illustrations and paintings, newspaper segments, and some letters of insight on the projects. This book is a necessity for Arts & Craft enthusiasts and an inspiration for new architectural students.

Gibbs Smith, Publisher
$34.95 U.S.
ISBN 1-58685-187-X
▣ 800.748.5439

THE NEW BUNGALOW
Essays by Matthew Bialecki, Christian Gladu, Jill Kessenich, Jim McCord, Su Bacon

The New Bungalow is a celebration of contemporary interpretations of Arts & Crafts design. It offers attractive, environmentally aware alternatives for today's housing. Founded on the principles of the original bungalow movement, it is a guide to creating a home that has a true, honest expression of style.

Gibbs Smith, Publisher
$39.95 U.S.
ISBN 1-58685-042-3
▣ 800.748.5439

Other books by Robbin Obomsawin from Gibbs Smith, Publisher that give practical advice and experience, helping take the dream of building a log home to reality.

LOG CABIN CLASSICS

Log cabin living is dreamed of by the romantic soul, and the imagination is the best tool for building a house with tree house charm. This book has twenty log cabin classics thoughtfully planned with soulful designs; they include an earthy blend and hearty mix of styles. *Log Cabin Classics* is not just décor but a way of life where simplicity in itself can be spectacular. This simple form of cabin architecture gives us the added time to dream bigger dreams.

$21.95 U.S.
ISBN 1-58685-315-5

SMALL LOG HOMES, STORYBOOK PLANS & ADVICE

Sage advice on building a handcrafted log home, as well as information on economy and space management in a small log home to avoid the feeling of being cramped. The book beautifully illustrates storybook log homes with fifteen classic floor plans. *Small Log Homes* is packed with useful information that helps sort through your wishes and dreams to build the perfect log home.

$21.95 U.S.
ISBN 1-58685-043-1

BEST LOG HOME PLANS

In this book, thirty of the most popular floor plans from top handcraft design professionals are showcased. Each thoughtfully planned home, incorporating distinctive quality and timeless design, takes the dreamer beyond the standard construction drawings and average floor plans to a place of builder/owner. The most often asked questions in the industry are addressed. *Best Log Home Plans* also takes you through what you must know about working with the contractor and design professional to keep your home building process efficient, with a clear and cost-effective form of communication with the trades.

$24.95 U.S.
ISBN 1-58685-146-2

GIBBS SMITH, PUBLISHER
▣ 800.748.5439

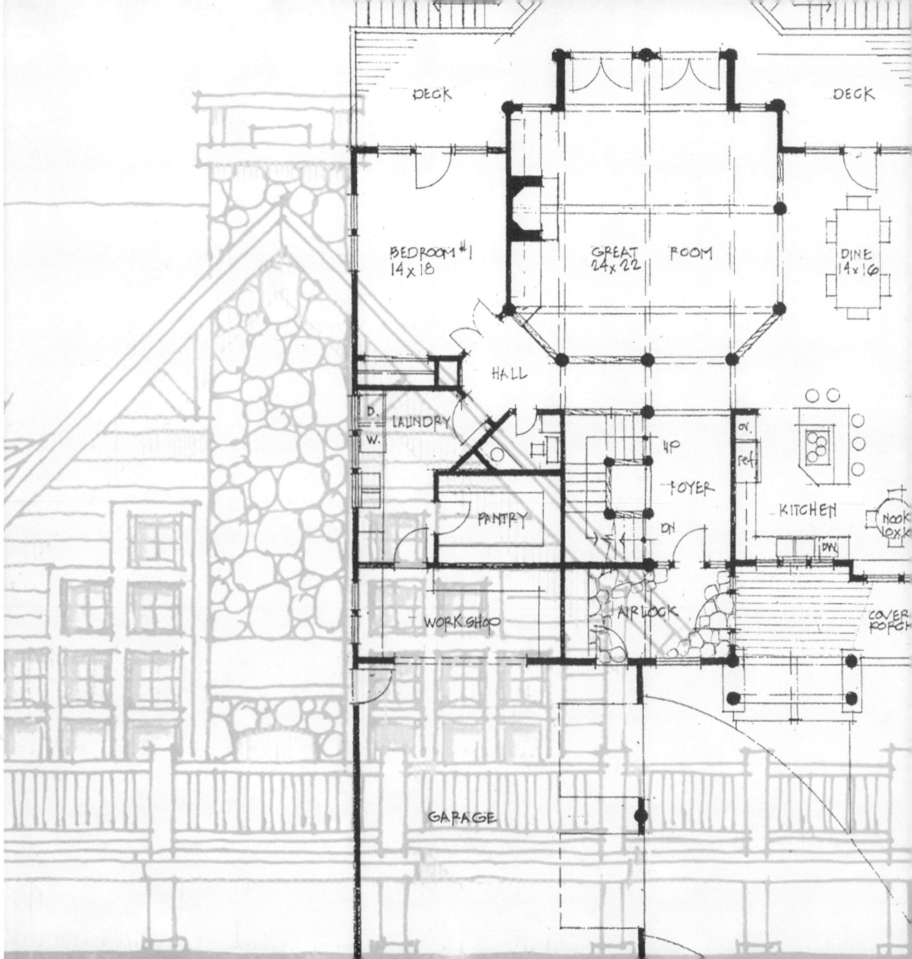

DECK

DECK

BEDROOM #1
14 x 18

GREAT   ROOM
24 x 22

DINE
14 x 16

HALL

D.

LAUNDRY

W.

ov.

ref.

40

FOYER

DN

KITCHEN

NOOK
10 x 10

PANTRY

WORKSHOP

AIRLOCK

COVER
PORCH

GARAGE

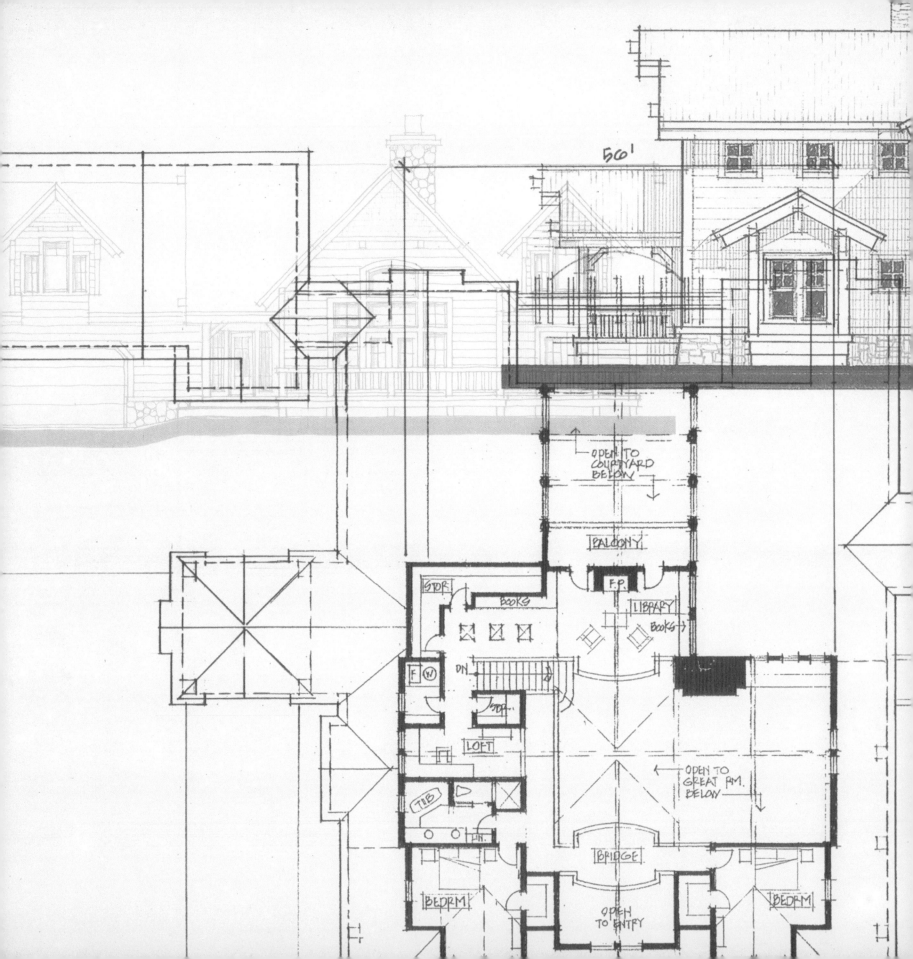

560'

OPEN TO
COURTYARD
BELOW

BALCONY

F.P.

STOR.

BOOKS

LIBRARY

BOOKS →

F W

DN

STOR

LOFT

OPEN TO
GREAT RM.
BELOW

TUB

LIN.

BRIDGE

BEDRM

OPEN
TO ENTRY

BEDRM